The
GIANT
Bathroom Book
of the
History of the
WORLD

The
GIANT
Bathroom Book
of the
History of the
WORLD

Magpie Books, London

Constable & Robinson Ltd
3 The Lanchesters
162 Fulham Palace Road
London W6 9ER

This edition published by Magpie Books,
an imprint of Constable & Robinson Ltd 2007

A copy of the British Library Cataloguing in Publication Data
is available from the British Library

ISBN 978-1-84529-750-3

Printed and bound in the European Union

3 5 7 9 10 8 6 4

Contents

Introduction

The Big Bang and All That   1

1

Miracle Workers Through the Ages   3

2

The Beginning of the World   29

3

Weird News – The Burning Mirror   37

4

The Dinosaurs   45

5

Scandalous Royal Tales   53

6

Stone-Age Man   89

7

Weird News – Christopher Columbus   97

8

Ancient Civilizations   105

9

Religious Mania   113

10

The Greeks   147

11

Weird News – Pirate Ladies   155

12

The Romans   163

13

Dumbology: Gaffes, Foul-Ups, Blunders, and Oddballs   171

14

Rock and Roll   215

vii

15

Messiahs, Fanatics, and Cults   223

16

Hollywood and the Movies   263

17

Weird News – Plot Against the King   271

18

The 20th Century   279

19

More Religious Mania   287

20

The First Millennium AD   317

21

Weird News – Silly Cycles   325

22

More Scandalous Royal Tales   331

23

Weird News – Death in Hammersmith   355

24

Yet More Religious Mania   363

25

Weird News – Living on a Tightrope   387

1

Introduction

The Big Bang and All That

Around 14 billion years ago, the universe began with the Big Bang. An entire universe, compressed into an infinitesimal space suddenly exploded in a fireball that eventually created the world as we know it today. Everything from human consciousness to reality TV, from the solar system and the wonders of the natural world to bubblegum pop music and Paris Hilton. All this derives from that one big bang.

Or does it? Some would beg to differ . . .

Perhaps the world was created in six days by a monotheistic God, who then rested on the seventh day, exhausted from the effort of planting fake dinosaur bones in the desert.

Or perhaps the world is cyclic and unchanging, always looping back to the same eternal state as the Vedas teach us, although if that's true, then what's the point of cleaning the house?

Perhaps the universe is a dream of a cosmic turtle god. Or perhaps we are simply being kept in vats, fooled by the hallucination visited on us by an evil demon who spent too much of his teenage years watching *The Matrix*?

It would be nice if we could start our history of the world with one unequivocal truth, but unfortunately we can't. Because everyone is still arguing about how the world started. Even those who believe in the Big Bang are still quibbling about the exact details. Was it big before it was a bang or was it a bang before it was big? And so on, ad infinitum.

And if we can't agree on how history began, what hope do we have of agreeing on anything else about the long story of mankind?

Luckily, in this book, we need not worry about such quibbles. All we need to know is that the universe started a long time ago, and then, when they were good and ready, humanity came along.

Humans spent their first few millennia fighting each other with clubs, as they hadn't yet figured out how to make guns and bombs. For a long time they were too busy fighting to write anything down, but eventually they invented reading and writing, to keep track of who was winning the most fights. The rest, as they say, is history.

In this book we have accumulated a selection of the most scurrilous, confusing, inane, and plain weird highlights from history. This isn't intended as a reliable, complete or impartial history. But perhaps it is in mankind's most ludicrous moments that we can see the clearest picture of the strange world we live in.

History isn't just made by great men and women. It's also made by fools, weirdos, philanderers, dullards, libertines, and freaks. And, for the most part, those are the subject of this book.

Welcome to an alternative history of the world . . .

Chapter One

Miracle Workers Through the Ages

The Messiah 700 BC

The word messiah means "anointed" in Hebrew, and refers to
the Jewish belief that King David will one day return and lead
his people to victory. (Christ means the same thing in Greek.)
The prophet Isaiah announced triumphantly that "unto us a child
is born", and that the Messiah would take the "government upon
his shoulders". Isaiah was writing roughly around 700 BC, after
the Assyrians had conquered Israel and led its people (including
the mythical "lost tribes") into exile. Ever since then, certain
men have become possessed of the conviction that they are the
promised Messiah, and ordered their disciples to follow them to
victory and kingship. None has so far succeeded.

The Great Pyramid Ancient Egypt

Some groups believe that the Great Pyramid in Egypt had
encoded within its measurements many great truths. Christian
sects have maintained that it was not the Egyptians who built it
at all but the Israelites. According to this theory the internal
passageways of the Pyramid, measured in the correct units, are a
three-dimensional model of the history of the world up to
Christ's birth. On a more secular level, twice the length of the
base of the Pyramid divided by its height, again in the correct
units, is supposed to approximate to *pi*. It is difficult to verify
these statements as the nature of the correct units is a matter of
conjecture, and the actual size of the Pyramid in any units is still
problematic.

The Anglo-Israelite fundamentalist sect took the argument a
stage further. Not only did the Egyptians not build the Pyramid;
it was also not entirely correct to say the Israelites built it.
According to the Anglo-Israelites, the Anglo-Saxon races of
Britain and America were the only true tribe of Israel remaining.
It was they who had built the Pyramid, as a warning that the

6

world would end and that Christ would return on 20 August 1953. When the date passed without significant upheaval, the Anglo-Israelites began to formulate the theory that the message of the Pyramid was not literal, but a religious metaphor.

Weird News Stories

HOW COOL?

The coldest place on earth is neither the North nor the South Pole, but Verkovank in Siberia, where a temperature of 100½ degrees below zero has been registered. The North pole is about 60½ below, while the South Pole often reaches 70½ below. North Dakota has also registered 70½ below.

The Millennium AD 1000

In the first millennium, it was widely believed that the year AD 1000 would mark the end of the world. It failed to materialize, but there was plenty of war and bloodshed – the Crusades, for example – to encourage the believers to feel that the end was nigh.

Off With His Head 12th Century

In 1172, an unnamed prophet from the Yemen was dragged in front of the Caliph, who demanded proof that he was a messenger from God. "That is easy," replied the prophet. "Cut off my head and I shall return to life." "That would indeed be a sign," said the Caliph, "and if you can do as you say, I will become your follower." At this point he signaled to one of his bodyguards. The head of the prophet rolled on the floor, and – predictably – the messiah failed to keep his promise.

Grisly Tales from History

Burn in Hell

In the twelfth century the Pope ordered that the Cathars be burned alive at the stake because they believed that the world was created by the devil.

The Flying Monk 17th Century

Giuseppe Desa was born in Apulia, Italy, in 1603. He was a strange, sickly boy who became known as "Open Mouth" because his mouth usually hung open. One commentator remarked that "he was not far from what today we should call a state of feeblemindedness"; a bishop described him as *idiota* (although the word meant innocent rather than idiotic). He was subject to "ecstasies" and, even as a teenager, given to ascetic self-torments that undermined his health.

At the age of seventeen he was accepted into the Capuchin order, but dismissed eight months later because of total inability to concentrate. Not long after, the order of Conventuals near Copertino accepted him as a stable boy, and at twenty-two he became a Franciscan priest. He continued to starve and flagellate himself, acquiring a reputation for holiness. Then one day, in the midst of his prayers after mass, he floated off the ground and landed on the altar in a state of ecstasy. He was unburned by candle flames, and flew back to his previous place.

Sent to see the Pope, he was again seized by such rapture that he rose in the air. His flying fits seem to have been always associated with the state that the Hindus called *samadhi,* ecstasy. His levitations ceased for two years when a hostile superior went out of his way to humiliate and persecute him, however, after a holiday in Rome and an enthusiastic reception by the people of Assisi, he regained his good spirits and sailed fifteen yards to embrace the image of the Virgin on the altar.

He seems to have been a curious but simple case; floating in the air when in a state of delight seems to have been his sole accomplishment. The ecstasy did not have to be religious; on one occasion, when shepherds were playing their pipes in church on Christmas Eve, he began to dance for sheer joy, then flew onto the high altar, without knocking over any of the burning candles. Oddly enough, Saint Joseph could control his flights. On one occasion, when he had flown past lamps and ornaments that blocked the way to the altar, his superior called him back, and he flew hack to the place he had vacated.

When a fellow monk remarked on the beauty of the sky, he shrieked and flew to the top of a nearby tree. He was also able to lift heavy weights; one story tells of how he raised a wooden cross that ten workmen were strugghng to place in position, and flew with it to the hole that had been prepared for it. He was also able to make others float. He cured a demented nobleman by seizing his hair and flying into the air with him, remaining there a quarter of an hour, according to his biographer; on another occasion, he seized a local priest by the hand, and after dancing around with him, they both flew, hand in hand. When on his deathbed, at the age of sixty, the doctor in attendance observed, as he cauterized a septic leg, that Father Joseph was floating in the air six inches above the chair. He died saying that he could hear the sounds and smell the scents of paradise.

Kings, dukes and philosophers witnessed his feats. When his canonization was suggested, the Church started an investigation into his flights, and hundreds of depositions were taken. He was proclaimed a saint a hundred and four years after his death.

CITY OF THE HORSE

Alexander the Great, besides Alexandria, also built a city called Bucephala, named after his horse Bucephalus, which was killed in battle in 326 BC.

The Miracles of Saint-Médard 18th Century

The strange events that took place in the little Paris churchyard of Saint-Médard between 1727 and 1732 sound so incredible, so preposterous, that the modern reader is tempted to dismiss them as pure invention. This would be a mistake, for an impressive mass of documents, including accounts by doctors, magistrates and other respectable public figures, attests to their genuineness. The miracles undoubtedly took place. But no doctor, philosopher or scientist has even begun to explain them.

They began with the burial of François de Pâris, the Deacon of Paris, in May 1727. François was only thirty-seven years old, yet he was revered as a holy man, with powers of healing. He was a follower of Bishop Cornelius Jansen, who taught that men could be saved only by divine grace, not by their own efforts.

The Deacon had no doubt whatever that his own healing powers came from God. Great crowds followed his coffin, many weeping. It was laid in a tomb behind the high altar of Saint-Médard.

Then the congregation filed past, laying their flowers on the corpse. A father supported his son, a cripple, as he leaned over the coffin. Suddenly, the child went into convulsions; he seemed to be having a fit. Several people helped to drag him, writhing, to a quiet corner of the church. Suddenly the convulsions stopped. The boy opened his eyes, looking around in bewilderment, and then slowly stood up. A look of incredulous joy crossed his face; then to the astonishment of the spectators he began to dance up and down, singing and laughing. His father found it impossible to believe, for the boy was using his withered right leg, which had virtually no muscles.

Later it was claimed that the leg had become as strong and normal as the other. The news spread. Within hours cripples, lepers, hunchbacks and blind men were rushing to the church. At first, few "respectable" people believed the stories of miraculous cures – the majority of the Deacon's followers were poor people. The rich preferred to leave their spiritual affairs in the hands of the Jesuits, who were more cultivated and worldly. But it soon became clear that ignorance and credulity could not be used as a blanket explanation for all the stories of marvels. Deformed limbs, it was said, were being straightened; hideous growths and cancers were disappearing without trace; horrible sores and wounds were healing instantly.

One of those who investigated happenings was a lawyer named Louis Adrien de Paige. When he told his friend, the magistrate Louis-Basile Carré de Montgéron, what he had seen, the magistrate assured him patronizingly that he had been taken in by conjuring tricks – the kind of "miracles" performed by

11

tricksters at fairgrounds. But he finally agreed to go with Paige
to the churchyard, if only for the pleasure of pointing out how
the lawyer had been deceived. They went there on the morning
of 7 September 1731. And de Montgéron left the churchyard a
changed man – he even endured prison rather than deny what he
had seen that day.

The first thing the magistrate saw when he entered the
churchyard was a number of women writhing on the ground,
twisting themselves to the most startling shapes, sometimes
bending backward until the backs of their heads touched their
heels. These ladies were all wearing a long cloth undergarment
that fastened around the ankles. Paige explained that this was
now obligatory for all women who wished to avail themselves
of the Deacon's miraculous powers. In the early days, when
women had stood on their heads or bent their bodies con-
vulsively, prurient young men had begun to frequent the
churchyard to view the spectacle.

Montgéron was shocked to see that some of the women and
girls were being sadistically beaten – at least, that is what at first
appeared to be going on. Men were striking them with heavy
pieces of wood and iron. Other women lay on the ground,
apparently crushed under immensely heavy weights. One girl
was naked to the waist: a man was gripping her nipples with a
pair of iron tongs and twisting them violently. Paige explained
that none of these women felt any pain; on the contrary, many
begged for more blows. And an incredible number of them were
cured of deformities or diseases by this violent treatment.

What Montgéron saw next finally shattered his resistance and
convinced him that he was witnessing something of profound
significance. A sixteen-year-old girl named Gabrielle Moler had
arrived, and the interest she excited made Montgéron aware that,
even among this crowd of miraculous freaks, she was a

celebrity. She removed her cloak and lay on the ground, her
skirt modestly round her ankles. Four men, each holding a
pointed iron bar, stood over her. When the girl smiled at them
they lunged down at her, driving their rods into her stomach.
Montgéron had to be restrained from interfering as the rods went
through the girl's dress and into her stomach. He looked for
signs of blood staining her dress. But none came, and the girl
looked calm and serene.

Next the bars were jarrred under her chin, forcing her head
back. It seemed inevitable that they would penetrate through to
her mouth; yet when the points were removed the flesh was
unbroken. The men took up sharp-edged shovels, placed them
against a breast, and then pushed with all their might; the girl
went on smiling gently. The breast, trapped between shovels,
should have been cut off, but it seemed impervious to the
assault. Then the cutting edge of a shovel was placed against her
throat, and the man wielding it did his best to cut off her head;
he did not seem to be able even to dent her neck.

Dazed, Montgéron watched as the girl was beaten with a
great iron truncheon shaped like a pestle. A stone weighing half
a hundredweight (25 kilograms) was raised ahove her body and
dropped repeatedly from a height of several feet. Finally,
Montgéron watched her kneel in front of a blazing fire, and
plunge her head into it. He could feel the heat from where he
stood; yet her hair and eyebrows were not even singed. When
she picked up a blazing chunk of coal and proceeded to eat it
Montgéron could stand no more and left.

But he went back repeatedly, until he had enough materials
for the first volume of an amazing book. He presented it to the
king, Louis XV, who was so shocked and indignant that he had
Montgéron thrown into prison. Yet Montgéron felt he had to
"bear witness", and was to publish two more volumes following

his release, full of precise scientific testimony concerning the miracles.

In the year following Montgéron's imprisonment, 1732, the Paris authorities decided that the scandal was becoming unbearable and closed down the churchyard. But the *convulsionnaires* had discovered that they could perform their miracles anywhere, and they continued for many years. A hardened sceptic, the scientist La Condamine, was as startled as Montgéron when, in 1759, he watched a girl named Sister Françoise being crucified on a wooden cross, nailed by the hands and feet over a period of several hours, and stabbed in the side with a spear. He noticed that all this obviously hurt the girl, and her wounds bled when the nails were removed; but she seemed none the worse for an ordeal that would have killed most people.

Weird News Stories

WHAT DID THE ROMANS EVER DO FOR US?

The bagpipes were first introduced into Scotland by the ancient Romans.

? ! ? ! ? ! ? ! ? ! ? ! ? ! ?

FASCINATING FACTS

Walled In, Dynasties of Ancient China

In 400 BC the Chinese began building the Grand Canal and the Great Wall. The Great Wall is 4,000 miles long and took 2,000 years to build as each Emperor added a bit more. However, it is not visible from space as is popularly thought. Each Emperor would build more because they wanted to take the credit for "finishing it". In fact, several walls, referred to as the Great Wall of China, have been built since the fifth century BC. The most famous one is the one built between 220 BC and 200 BC by the first Emperor of China, Qin Shi Huang; this wall was located much further north than the current wall as we know it, built during the Ming Dynasty, and little of it remains.

The Great Wall is the world's longest man-made structure, stretching over approximately 6,400 km (4,000 miles) from Shanhai Pass in the east to Lop Nur in the west, along an arc that roughly delineates the southern edge of Inner Mongolia.

? ! ? ! ? ! ? ! ? ! ? ! ? ! ?

The Day of Judgement According to William Miller
12th Century

On 22 October 1843, crowds of men and women gathered on a hilltop in Massachusetts, led by their prophet William Miller. In the previous year, Miller, a farmer and an ardent student of the *Book of Daniel,* had arrived at the conclusion that the end of the world was at hand, and that Christ was about to return to earth. One man tied a pair of turkey wings to his shoulders and climbed a tree to be ready for his ascent into heaven; unfortunately, he fell down and broke his arm. Other disciples carried umbrellas to aid the flight. One woman had tied herself to her trunk so that it would accompany her as she sailed upward.

When midnight passed with no sign of Armageddon, the disciples ruefully went home. One farmer had given his farm to his son – who was a non-believer, and who now declined to give it back. Most of the others had sold all they had. In this moment of depression, Miller suddenly had an inspiration: his calculations had been based on the Christian year, and no doubt he should have used the Jewish year. That would make the date of Armageddon the following 22 March. On that date, his followers once more gathered for the last Trumpet. Still nothing happened.

One man wrote sadly: "Still in the cold world! No deliverance – the Lord did not come." Miller's 50,000 followers soon dwindled to a small band of "true believers". Miller himself was not among them; he admitted sorrowfully that he had made his mistake through pride and fanaticism. Another follower made an even more penetrating comment, which might be regarded as the epitaph of any number of "messiahs": "We were deluded by mere human influence, which we mistook for the Spirit of God."

Drunk and Disorderly in the thirteenth century

Middle Ages

In medieval times, it seems that the favourite adult recreation was undoubtedly drinking. Both men and women gathered in the "tavern", although the term often meant the house of a neighbour who had recently brewed a batch of ale, going cheap at the price of three gallons for a penny. Apparently, accidents, quarrels, and acts of violence often followed a session of drinking, in the thirteenth century as well as subsequent ones. The rolls of the royal coroners, reporting fatal accidents, have many such incidents.

In 1276 in Elstow, Osbert le Wuayl, son of William Cristmasse, was coming home sometime around midnight. He is described as being "drunk and disgustingly over-fed," after an evening out in Bedford. He fell and fatally struck his head on a stone "breaking the whole of his head." In another account, a man stumbled off his horse riding home from the tavern and it trampled him to death.

Another man fell into a well in the marketplace and was drowned. Other tales include a report of a man who relieved himself in the local pond, fell in, and drowned while another was bitten by a dog while carrying a pot of ale down the village street. He is said to have tripped while picking up a stone to throw at the dog, and fatally struck his head against a wall. There is also an account of a child who slipped from her drunken mother's lap into a pan of hot milk on the hearth.

The Death of Joanna Southcott 19th Century

Sometimes, the prophet – or prophetess – loses faith at the last moment, but even when that happens, the disciples remain immune to doubt. When the English prophetess Joanna Southcott lay on her deathbed in 1814, she suddenly announced to her dismayed followers that her life's work now appeared a delusion. Although Joanna was a virgin, she had been convinced that she was about to give birth to the "child" foretold by Isaiah. And when one of her followers reminded her that she was carrying the Messiah (called Shiloh) in her womb, Joanna's tears suddenly changed to smiles.

After her death a few days later, her followers kept her body warm for three days as she had instructed them – then summoned a small army of medical men to remove the Christ child from her womb. The smell of putrefying flesh filled the room as the surgeon made the first incision, and some of the disciples hastily lit pipes to cover the smell. But when the womb was opened there was obviously no baby there.

"Damn me", said a doctor, "if the child is not *gone.*" These words filled the disciples with new hope. Obviously, he meant that the child had been there, but had now been transferred to heaven. And even today, there are a small number of followers of Joanna Southcott – they call themselves the Panacea Society – who believe that when her mysterious box is opened – a box supposed to contain her secret writings – all sin and wickedness in the world will suddenly disappear.

18

Weird News Stories

A WOMAN'S PLACE?

The word "lady" derives from the Old English "hlaefdige" – which literally means: "loaf-kneader."

The Crucifixion of Margaret Peter 19th Century

Women have also been among these prophets of the new Millennium, and a few have shown even greater fanaticism than their male counterparts. Perhaps the most gruesome example is the German prophetess Margaret Peter. In the week after Easter 1823, a horrible ceremony took place in a house in Wildisbuch, on the German-Swiss border. A twenty nine-year-old woman named Margaret Peter, who was regarded as a holy woman by her disciples, announced that she had decided that she had to be crucified if Satan was to be defeated. Her sister Elizabeth immediately begged to be allowed to take her place. To demonstrate her sincerity, she picked up a mallet and struck herself on the head with it. Margaret then shouted: "It has been revealed to me that Elizabeth shall sacrifice herself," and she hit her sister on the head with a hammer. Then the remaining ten people in the room – including Margaret's other brothers and sisters – proceeded to beat Elizabeth with crowbars, hammers and wedges. "Don't worry," Margaret shouted, "I will raise her from the dead." One tremendous blow finally shattered Elizabeth's skull.

"Now *I* must die," Margaret told them. "You must crucify me." Following her sister's example, she picked up a hammer and hit herself on the head, then ordered the others to make a cross out of loose floorboards. When it was ready, she sent her sister Susanna downstairs to fetch nails. When Susanna returned, Margaret was lying on the floor on the cross. "Nail me to it," she ordered. "Don't be afraid. I will rise in three days." Two followers obediently nailed her elbows to the cross. The sight of the blood made them hesitate, and one was sick. Margaret encouraged them. "I feel no pain. Go on. Drive a nail through my heart." They drove nails through both her breasts, and a girl called Ursula tried to drive a knife through her heart. It bent against one of her ribs. Her brother Conrad, unable to stand the sight any longer, picked up a hammer and smashed in her skull.

The ten remaining disciples then went to eat their midday meal. They were exhausted but had no doubt that Margaret and Elizabeth would be among them again in three days' time. The deaths had taken place on Saturday; that meant Margaret and Elizabeth were due to arise on Tuesday.

But as the disciples sat around the battered corpses on Tuesday morning, no sign of life answered their prayers. Meanwhile, the local pastor, who had heard about the "sacrifice" from another disciple, called in the police. (He had known about the deaths for two days, but felt he had to give Margaret time to make good her promise.) The disciples were arrested, and taken to prison. They were tried in Zurich that December, and were all sentenced to varying prison terms.

Grisly Tales from History

Black Death

Middle Ages

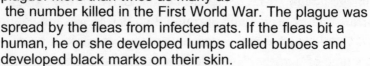

Between the years 1346 and 1350, twenty-five million people in Europe (approximately one third of the population), died from the Black Death, now known as the bubonic plague. More than twice as many as the number killed in the First World War. The plague was spread by the fleas from infected rats. If the fleas bit a human, he or she developed lumps called buboes and developed black marks on their skin.

Rasputin, "the Holy Sinner" 19th–20th Century

Grigory Rasputin's body was taken from the frozen River Neva, in Petrograd, on 1 January 1917. He had been murdered three days before, and was one of the most notorious figures in Russia. Now that he was dead, he would become a legend all over the world – a symbol of evil, cunning, and lust. Most stories about Rasputin are full of lurid details of how Rasputin spent his days in drunken carousing, his nights in sexual debauchery. They tell us how he deceived the Tsar and Tsarina into thinking he was a miracle worker and how he was the evil genius who brought about the Russian Revolution and the downfall of the Romanov dynasty. It is all untrue. Yet it makes such a good story that there is little chance that Rasputin will ever receive justice. The truth about him is that he really was a miracle worker and a man of strange powers. He was certainly no saint – very few magicians are – and tales of his heavy drinking and sexual prowess are undoubtedly based on fact. But he was no diabolical schemer.

Rasputin was born in the village of Pokrovskoe in 1870. His
father was a fairly well-to-do peasant. As a young man,
Rasputin had a reputation for wildness until he visited a
monastery and spent four months there in prayer and meditation.
For the remainder of his life, he was obsessed by religion. He
married at nineteen and became a prosperous carter. Then the
call came again; he left his family and took to the road as a kind
of wandering monk. When eventually he returned, he was a
changed man, exuding an extraordinarily powerful magnetism.
The young people of his village were fascinated by him. He
converted one room in his house into a church, and it was
always full. The local priest became envious of his following,
however, and Rasputin was forced to leave home again.

Rasputin had always possessed the gift of second sight. One
day during his childhood, this gift had revealed to him the
identity of a peasant who had stolen a horse and hidden it in a
barn. Now, on his second round of travels, he also began to
develop extraordinary healing powers. He would kneel by the
beds of the sick and pray; then he would lay hands on them, and
cure many of them. When he came to St Petersburg, probably
late in 1903, he already had a reputation as a wonder worker.
Soon he was accepted in aristocratic society in spite of his rough
peasant manners.

It was in 1907 that he suddenly became the power behind the
throne. Three years before, Tsarina Alexandra had given birth to
a longed-for heir to the throne, Prince Alexei. But it was soon
apparent that Alexei had inherited haemophilia, a disease that
prevents the blood from clotting, and from which a victim may
bleed to death even with a small cut. At the age of three the
prince fell and bruised himself so severely that an internal
haemorrhage developed. He lay in a fever for days, and doctors
despaired of his life. Then the Tsarina recalled the man of God

she had met two years earlier, and sent for Rasputin. As soon as he came in he said calmly: "Do not worry the child. He will be all right." He laid his hand on the boy's forehead sat down on the edge of the bed, and began to talk to him in a quiet voice. Then he knelt and prayed. In a few minutes the boy was in a deep and peaceful sleep, and the crisis was over.

Henceforward the Tsarina felt a powerful emotional dependence on Rasputin – a dependence nourished by the thinly veiled hostility with which Alexandra, a German, was treated at court. Rasputin's homely strength brought her a feeling of security. The Tsar also began to confide in Rasputin, who became a man of influence at court. Nicholas II was a poor ruler, not so much cruel as weak, and too indecisive to stem the rising tide of social discontent. His opponents began to believe that Rasputin was responsible for some of the Tsar's reactionary policies, and a host of powerful enemies began to gather. On several occasions the Tsar had to give way to the pressure and order Rasputin to leave the city. On one such occasion, the young prince fell and hurt himself again. For several days he tossed in agony, until he seemed too weak to survive. The Tsarina dispatched a telegram to Rasputin, and he telegraphed back: "The illness is not as dangerous as it seems." From the moment it was received, the prince began to recover.

World War I brought political revolution and military catastrophe to Russia. Its outbreak was marked by a strange coincidence: Rasputin was stabbed by a madwoman at precisely the same moment as the Archduke Franz Ferdinand was shot at Sarajevo.

Rasputin hated war, and might have been able to dissuade the Tsar from leading Russia into the conflict. But he was in bed recovering from his stab wound when the moment of decision came. Conspirators planned Rasputin's end in the last days of

1916. Prince Felix Yussupov, a man he trusted, lured him to a cellar. After feeding him poisoned cakes, Yussupov shot him in the back; then Rasputin was beaten with an iron bar. Such was his immense vitality that he was still alive when the murderers dropped him through the hole in the ice into the Neva River.

Among his papers was found a strange testament addressed to the Tsar. It stated that he had a strong feeling he would die by violence before 1 January 1917, and that if peasants killed him, the Tsar would reign for many years to come. However, if he were killed by aristocrats – as he was – then "none of your children or relations will remain alive for more than two years." He was right. The Tsar and his family were all murdered in July 1918 – an amazing example, among many, of Rasputin's gift of precognition.

Weird News Stories

THREE TIMES A LADY

There was one queen of England who never even saw her realm. She was the wife of Richard the Lionheart, Queen Berengaria, daughter of Sancho VI of Navarre. They were married in Cyprus in May 1191. The King's wanderings meant that she saw him only twice more; she lived in France and Italy and died in Le Mans, about 1230.

A Miraculous Cure 20th Century

Josephine Hoare, a healthy girl of twenty-one, had been married for only six months when she developed chronic nephritis, a serious inflammation of the kidneys. Her family was told that she had no more than two years to live. At her mother's suggestion, she was taken to Lourdes. At the famous French shrine, Josephine braved the icy waters of the spring. Although she felt peaceful, she was not conscious of any change. When she went home, however, her doctor said in amazement that the disorder seemed to have cleared. Her swollen legs returned to normal size, her blood pressure became normal, and her energy increased. But she was warned that pregnancy would certainly cause a relapse.

Several years passed. Then Josephine and her husband had the opportunity to revisit Lourdes; and Josephine lit a candle of thanksgiving. Soon after they got home she felt a sharp pain in her back. Fearful that nephritis was recurring, she went to her doctor. His diagnosis was simply that she was six months pregnant – and she had had no relapse.

Josephine Hoare had her baby, a son, and remained in good health. For her and her family, the spring of Lourdes had produced a double miracle.

A Hairy Tale 20th Century

Does a place of worship have more intense thought fields than ordinary buildings? Can this explain the incredible case of the doll with human hair that keeps on growing?

The story comes from northern Japan and started in 1938. In that year Eikichi Suzuki took a ceramic doll to the temple in the village of Monji-Saiwai Cho for safekeeping. It had been a treasured possession of his beloved sister Kiku, who had died nineteen years before at the age of three. Suzuki kept it carefully in a box with the ashes of his dead sister.

Suzuki went off to the Second World War and didn't return for the doll until 1947. When he opened the box in the presence of the priest, they discovered that the doll's hair had grown down to its shoulders. A skin specialist from the Hokkaido University medical faculty said it was human hair.

The doll was placed on the altar, and its hair continued to grow. It is still growing, and is now almost waist length. The temple has become a place of pilgrimage for worshippers who believe the doll is a spiritual link with Buddha.

The priest of Monji-Saiwai Cho thinks that the little girl's soul somehow continues to live through the doll she loved so much.

Weird News Stories

EAT YOUR WORDS

In 1644, Danish author Theodore Reinking was given the choice of eating his own book or being executed. King Christian IV of Denmark thought the book too democratic in sentiment. Reinking chose to eat the book torn up in his soup.

Search for a Missing Boy 20th Century

In 1933 a six-year-old boy vanished from his home in Miège in the Swiss Alps. After an unsuccessful search for the boy, the town's mayor wrote to Abbé Mermet, who had often assisted police in locating missing people. The Abbé needed an article used by the missing person, a description of the last place he or she was seen, and a map of the surrounding area to do his work. He used a pendulum and a form of dowsing to find the missing person.

After the Abbé applied his pendulum to the problem of the missing boy, he reported that the child had been carried away into the mountains by a large bird of prey, probably an eagle. He also said that the bird – although enormous – had dropped its load twice to rest and regain its strength.

There was no trace of the boy at the first place the Abbé indicated. A recent heavy snowfall prevented a thorough search at the second place, but the conclusion was that Abbé Mermet had made a mistake.

When the snow melted two weeks later, however; a gang of woodcutters found the torn and mangled body of a small boy. It was the missing child. The bird had apparently been prevented from completely savaging the child's body by the sudden heavy storm that had also hidden the forlorn evidence.

Scientific investigation established that the boy's shoes and clothes had not come into contact with the ground where the body was found. He could only have reached the remote spot by air – the pitiful victim of the bird of prey. Later the boy's father apologized to the Abbé for having doubted him.

Living on the Land

Middle Ages

In the Middle Ages most people worked on the land and they were very poor. The average life span of a peasant was only twenty-five years. The Lord of the Manor owned the land and the peasants worked the land for him. As payment the peasants received a small plot of land on which they could grow their own food. Even so, a portion of this had to be given to the lord as a tax. The lord was the only one with a mill capable of grinding corn for flour. Many banned the peasants from using hand mills so that they had to use the lord's mill and pay for using it. Mostly, the lord would use the money for large feasts.

WEIRD TALES

Atlantis

Atlantis, the fabled lost continent, is first mentioned in Plato's dialogues between *Timaeus and Critias* written around 350 BC. There it is described as an enormous island "beyond the Pillars of Hercules" (the Straits of Gibraltar). On this island, civilization flourished long before Athens was founded in 9600 BC. The inhabitants were great engineers and aggressive warriors, harassing early European and Asian civilization until the Athenians finally conquered them on their own territory. At that point great floods overwhelmed the island, and both the Athenian army and the Atlantean civilization disappeared beneath the ocean in a day and a night.

Plato describes their culture and territory in detail. The city was eleven miles in diameter, formed from concentric rings of land and water. The Atlanteans were fed by crops grown on a large plain 230 by 340 miles located behind the city. Plato describes their buildings and their habits, setting the pattern for all future Utopian literature; indeed that is all that his writings on Atlantis were considered to be for roughly two thousand years.

In 1882, Ignatius Donnelly, American senator and well-read theorist published a book suggesting that Plato's "fable" was based upon a real civilization. Much of the minutiae of Donnelly's argument proves to be inaccurate on close examination, but the idea that there was an entirely lost civilization beneath the waves proved too romantic to be stifled.

Atlantis has been associated with Lyoness, the sunken area of land between Land's End in Cornwall and the Isles of Scilly. Regular patterns of stones and carvings found on the sea bed near Bimini in the Bahamas have also been identified as Atlantean.

The story of Atlantis still fascinates, but without more positive evidence it must be regarded as more a cautionary tale than a historical treatise.

Chapter Two

A Brief, Unreliable History of . . .

The Beginning of the World

The Beginning of the World

Everything you ever wanted to know about what happened after the Big Bang.

1

If scientists are right that the world started with a big bang, the first few years must have been a pretty chaotic time. Huge chunks of rock zooming around in space, not much fun to be had . . .

2

Eventually some swirling balls of gas and rock started to form. At this stage the universe looked a little bit like a very bad goth rock gig, with a lot of dry ice and flashing lights, and some terrible, inexplicable noise.

3

These swirling balls of gas started to squeeze themselves into dense, very hot masses. Then someone hit the ignition button and stars were formed.

4

The solar system was probably formed after a supernova exploded nearby. A huge spinning disc, not unlike a roller disco, was formed, and gradually resolved itself into a single sun surrounded by a series of increasingly strange planets.

5

The solar system has eight planets, 169 moons, four dwarf planets (including Pluto) and a lot of other space junk, including asteroids, comets, the Kuiper belt and, because no one has done much cleaning in the last few billion years, a heck of a lot of interplanetary dust.

6

It's hard to say how life on earth started. Maybe this is the best argument for believing in a God, or maybe it just happened. One thing we do know is that, like Goldilocks choosing her porridge, the Earth is the best planet in the Solar System for sustaining life because it is neither too hot nor too cold.

7

We know from many films and books that Mars was also teeming with life at one point, though whether it was inhabited by little green men, giant space slugs, Klingons or just tiny little bacteria is still a matter of debate.

8

Earth at this stage was basically a big, steaming swamp. We had water, seasons, oxygen, and sunsets, but as yet there was no one to enjoy all these amenities.

9

On Earth, a few little organisms started to wriggle and evolve. Starting from a few simple cells, they joined together, and grew useful accessories such as hands, feet, eyes, fins, horns, and antennae.

10

And now the party was finally about to start. Little things began to wriggle, crawl, fly, and boogie all over the world. The steam from the swamps started to clear, the oceans receded from the land, and a beautiful blue and green planet emerged, just waiting for mankind to come and despoil it . . .

35

Future Bingo

The future history of the world is hard to predict. But as we look forward in fear and hope, why not have some fun while we're waiting?

Keep this **Future Bingo** sheet to hand, and cross off any events that actually happen in the future. If you get a full page of amazing future events, then shout out "House".

If you send the finished page to the **Future Bingo** corporation (at an address yet to be determined), you may even receive a mystery prize . . .

"American Pie" adopted as USA's national anthem.	New Zealand declares war on Latvia in response to "snide comments by Latvian ambassador."
Carjacking accepted as an Olympic sport.	Eiffel Tower revealed as alien transmitter.
Hurricane Elvis destroys Mount Rushmore.	Chicken beaks become official world currency.

Chapter Three

Weird News: The Burning Mirror

Sometime between 215 BC and 212 BC, the ancient Greek
mathematician and inventor Archimedes is said to have
destroyed the Roman fleet that was besieging Syracuse by using
a "burning mirror". The tale is recorded in detail in Anthemius's
sixteenth-century *Remarkable Devices* and there are also
references in Polybius, Plutarch and Lucian's *Hippias*, but
until now there has been no other evidence to support its
actuality.

Dr Ioannis Sakkas has long held an interest in the fable and
set about devising how the sage might have made a primitive
laser with the technology of the time.

"Archimedes may have employed flat bronze mirrors, the size
of large shields, from the walls of the city to concentrate the
solar energy and set the galleys on fire," Dr Sakkas said. "The
flat mirrors are, for this purpose, the most practical as they can
be handled by men obeying commands. You can visualize the
scene: the Roman ships would hold as they converged on the
sixty-foot-high walls of Syracuse within bowshot. The element
of surprise was probably crucial, since the target had to be static.
The defenders with their shield-like mirrors would focus the
reflection of the sun on each galley and set it on fire in
seconds."

At the Scaramanga naval base, Dr Sakkas used fifty or sixty
sailors to wield mirrors made of bronze-coated glass, each
measuring five feet by three feet. The men stood in a line along
a narrow pier 130 feet from the target and moved their mirrors
as ordered. The target was a six-foot rowing boat with an outline
of a galley made of tarred plywood – a slow burning material –
attached to the landward side. "The reflective power would be
about one-tenth less than the polished bronze Archimedes would
have used, and the sun today is fairly weak," explained the
doctor. Nevertheless, once all the mirrors were beaming at it, the

galley cut-out was burning after only two minutes. "The heat generated today must have ranged between 280 and 340 degrees centigrade," estimated Dr Sakkas.

Weird News Stories

HUGH WILLIAMS

On 5 December 1664, a man named Hugh Williams was the only survivor of a boat that sank crossing the Menai Strait – between Anglesey and Carnarvonshire in Wales. On 5 December 1785, the sole survivor of another such accident was also called Hugh Williams; sixty other passengers were drowned. On 5 August 1820, a man named Hugh Williams was again the sole survivor out of twenty-six passengers.

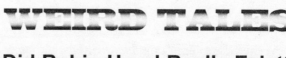

WEIRD TALES

Did Robin Hood Really Exist?

The Hobby Horse ceremony takes place on May Day (1 May) in Padstow, Cornwall, England. Its purpose is to suggest that Robin Hood was really called Robin Wood, and that his name is derived from the Norse god Woden. In fact, he appears as Robin Wood in T. H. White's *The Sword in the Stone*, in which he becomes a contemporary of King Arthur, who (if he ever existed) was said to have died about AD 540.

Those who assume there is no smoke without fire are

inclined to believe that Robin Hood was a real outlaw who at some time lived in Sherwood Forest, who became so popular during his own lifetime that he soon became the subject of tales and ballads. Yet it seems unlikely that he was around as early as Richard the Lionheart (1157–99), or he would surely have been mentioned in manuscripts before Piers Plowman two centuries later. In his *Chronicle of Scotland*, written about 1420, Andrew Wyntoun refers to Robin Hood and Little John for the year 1283, which sounds altogether more likely – about a century before Piers Plowman.

One of the most important clues to Robin's identity emerged in the mid-nineteenth century, when the Historic Documents Commission was cataloguing thousands of documents that represented eight centuries of British history. It was in 1852 that the antiquary Joseph Hunter claimed that he had stumbled upon a man who sounded as if he might be the original Robin Hood.

His name, in fact, was Robert, and he was the son of Adam Hood, a forester in the service of the Earl de Warenne. (Robin was simply a diminutive of Robert – not, in those days, a name in its own right.) He was born about 1280, and on 25 January 1316 Robert Hood and his wife Matilda paid two shillings for permission to take a piece of the earl's waste ground in "Bickhill" (or Bitchhill) in Wakefield. It was merely the size of a kitchen garden – thirty feet long by sixteen feet wide. The rent for this was sixpence a year. The Manor Court Roll for 1357 shows a house "formerly the property of Robert Hode" on the site – so by that time Robert Hood was presumably dead.

After his coronation (in 1307) Edward II dismissed his father's ministers and judges and made his lover, Piers Gaveston, Earl of Cornwall – to the fury of his barons. It was the most powerful of these, Thomas, Earl of Lancaster, who forced Edward to accept the rule of twenty-eight barons (called Ordainers), and who finally executed Piers Gaveston in 1312. Edward's lack of attention to affairs of state allowed the Scots – against whom his father Edward I had fought so successfully – to throw off their English masters.

Edward II was defeated at Bannockburn in 1314, two years before Robert Hood hired the piece of waste ground and set up. Lancaster's army was defeated at Boroughbridge on 16 March 1322, and Lancaster was captured and beheaded. Many of Lancaster's supporters were declared outlaws, and their property confiscated. There is a document stating that a "building of five rooms" on Bickhill, Wakefield, was among the property confiscated. Many believe that this was Robert Hood's home, and that the outlaw now took refuge in the nearby forest of Barnsdale, where he soon became a highly successful robber.

It is of course conceivable that the Robin Hood who lived in Edward's reign had no connection with the legendary outlaw of Sherwood Forest. One reference book (*Who's Who In History*) says that he was alive in 1230, in the reign of Henry III. Records show that the Sheriff of Yorkshire sold his possessions in that year (for 32s 6d) when he became an outlaw; but the same reference book admits that the Robyn Hode of Wakefield is also a good contender.

There is something to be said for this earlier dating, for it would give more time for the legend of Robin Hood to spread throughout England. But there is also a great deal to be said for Robin Hood of Wakefield. If he became an outlaw in 1322, as a result of the Lancaster rebellion, then he spent only one year in Sherwood Forest before the king pardoned him. The story of his pardon by the homosexual king certainly rings true – as does his appointment as a gentleman of the bedchamber. It is natural to speculate that he may have found that his duties in the bedchamber involved more than he had bargained for, although at this time the king's favourite was the younger Hugh le Despenser (executed by Mortimer and Isabella in 1326). So he returned to the green wood, and became a hero of legend.

We do not know whether he became the arch-enemy of the Sheriff of Nottingham, but the sheriff (an old-fashioned Police Chief) would have been responsible for law and order in Nottinghamshire and South Yorkshire, and would certainly have resented a band of outlaws who lived off the king's deer. One chronicle states that Robin also had a retreat in what became known as Robin Hood's Bay, and ships in which he could escape to sea. (He is also said to have operated as far afield as Cumberland.) If a concerted attempt had been made to flush him out, it would probably have succeeded. But most of the peasants and tenant farmers would have been on Robin's side. There had been a time when the forests of England were common land, and half-starved peasantry must have felt it was highly unreasonable that thousands of square miles of forest should be reserved for the king's hunting, when the king could not make use of a fraction of that area.

Robin Hood was buried in the grounds of the nunnery, within a bowshot of its walls. *Grafton's Chronicle* (1562) says he was buried under an inscribed stone, and a century later another chronicle reported that his tomb, with a plain cross on a flat stone, could be seen in the cemetery. In 1665 Dr Nathaniel Johnstone made a drawing of it; *Gough's Sepulchral Monuments* also has an engraving of the tombstone. In the early nineteenth century navvies building a railway broke up the stone – it is said they believed its chips to be a cure for toothache. So the last trace of the real existence of Robin Hood disappeared.

The real significance of Robin Hood is that he lived in a century when the peasants were beginning to feel an increasing resentment about their condition. This resentment expressed itself in the revolutionary doctrines of John Ball and exploded in the Peasants' Revolt of 1381, only a short time after Robin is first mentioned in print by Langland. The Peasants' Revolt is generally considered to mark the end of the Middle Ages, but it is in the ballads and myths surrounding Robin Hood that we can see that the state of mind known as the Middle Ages is coming to an end.

Weird News Stories

MINI MEALS

Oswaldus Norhingerus, who lived in the time of Shakespeare, specialized in carving miniature objects out of ivory. He once carved 16,000 table utensils so small that they could be accommodated in a cup the size of a coffee bean. Each dish was almost invisible to the naked eye, yet perfect in every detail. Pope Paul V viewed them through a powerful pair of spectacles.

Chapter Four

A Brief, Unreliable History of . . .
The Dinosaurs

The Beginning of the World

Everything you ever wanted to know about
the biggest creatures to ever walk the earth.

1

Dinosaurs were around for a pretty long time, from about 230
million years ago to about 65 million years ago. For that time they
pretty much ruled the world – they were ugly and stupid, but they
were also very, very big, so no one liked to argue with them.

2

The word dinosaur means "terrible lizard". Technically,
dinosaurs weren't lizards at all , but if you met some on a dark
night you could be forgiven for thinking they were, if you
survived long enough to think about it.

3

We know a lot about dinosaur skeletons – we have reconstucted
the remains of dinosaurs large and small all over the world to
put them in museums so we can scare small children with them.
What we don't know is what dinosaurs really looked like. They
are often pictured with leathery, scaly skin – but it's equally
possible that they had feathers, or fur or something else
altogether. You may prefer to imagine them being pink with
purple polka dots.

4

Some dinosaurs ate nothing but grass and vegetation; others ate small animals. The really scary ones, like Tyrannosaurus Rex, ate other dinosaurs.

5

The biggest dinosaur we know of was Brachiosaurus Brancai (also known as the Giraffatitan because of its long neck) which was about 40 feet tall and 75 feet long. He (or she) probably weighed about 50 tons, so was banned from walking across bridges. Even little dinosaurs were pretty big – the concept that "small is beautiful" wasn't developed until later in the history of the world.

6

There were all kinds of dinosaurs, including swimming ones (ichthyosaurs) and flying ones (pterosaurs). Technically these don't count as dinosaurs, but if you had a dinosaur party, it was better to just let them in rather than making a scene about it.

7

No one knows for sure why the dinosaurs became extinct, but the most likely theory is that a comet or large asteroid collided with the earth, causing a huge natural catastrophe that the dinosaurs couldn't survive. Other theories include the idea that the earth's climate suffered a catastrophic change for other reasons, perhaps because the dinosaurs had started to drive around in SUVs and weren't recycling their bottles properly.

8

Birds are generally reckoned to be a modern survival of the dinosaur period. Birds may look cute and fluffy but deep down they are vicious creatures biding their time and waiting for a chance to take over the world once more.

9

Various books and films have depicted a land where dinosaurs survived the passage of time and exist in the modern world. Recently there was great excitement in the scientific community when the esteemed Dr Wanglestan claimed to have discovered such an enclave but on closer examination it was revealed that he had merely got lost in Washington DC and accidentally walked in on a Senate debate.

10

When the dinosaurs were wiped out by said comet, many small species of animals remained including insects, early reptiles, and some small money-like mammals, who survived by hiding in a tree hollow somewhere in Africa. Those little monkey creatures would go on to become the founders of the human race . . .

Future Bingo

The future history of the world is hard to predict. But as we look forward in fear and hope, why not have some fun while we're waiting?

Keep this **Future Bingo** sheet to hand, and cross off any events that actually happen in the future. If you get a full page of amazing future events, then shout out "House".

If you send the finished page to the **Future Bingo** corporation (at an address yet to be determined), you may even receive a mystery prize . . .

World peace achieved.	Nuclear fusion powers first human colony ship to Alpha Centauri.
American/Canada peace conference called by Middle East powers.	Triffids invade Moscow.
Loch Ness monster found in Lake Tahoe.	Worlds biggest daisy chain longer than Wall of China.

Chapter Five

Scandalous Royal Tales

The Murder of King Tut 1500 BC

Rumours have always circulated that King "Tut" (Tutankhamen) was murdered. Tutankhamen lived, ruled, and died 3,000 years ago. A later pharaoh tried to erase him from Egyptian history so, until the rediscovery of his tomb in 1922, little was known about him. We don't know for sure who Tutankhamen's parents were. He was probably the son of the pharaoh Akhenaten and his secondary wife, Kiya. Egyptian kings often had more than one wife at a time, and Akhenaten's most important wife, or "Great Wife," was the famous beauty Nefertiti. Apparently Akhenaten and Nefertiti had six daughters (one of whom may also have become Akhenaten's wife!).

Tutankhamen's mother seems to have died giving birth to him and when Tutankhamen was just ten years old, Akhenaten also died. Young, inexperienced Tutankhamen was now the pharaoh of Egypt. He quickly abandoned Amarna, returned to Egypt's traditional capital, Thebes, and resumed the worship of the old gods. He also married his half-sister Ankhesenamen, who was about his age. We have no way of knowing how Tutankhamen felt about the abandonment of his childhood home and religion, but his marriage seems to have been a very happy one. Paintings and objects in the Tutankhamen's tomb show the affection between the young husband and wife. Ankhesenamen offers her husband flowers; Tutankhamen pours perfume into his wife's hands. Also found in the tomb were the mummies of two fetuses, apparently children miscarried by Ankhesenamen. It seems Tutankhamen and his wife had no surviving children.

At the age of eighteen, Tutankhamen suddenly died. There are no historical records explaining the cause or circumstances of his death. However, some historians claim that X-rays show that a blow to the head might have killed the young pharaoh. More suspicion is raised by what happened after Tutankhamen's death. His widow sent desperate messages to the king of the Hittites, Egypt's enemies, begging him to let her marry one of his sons. She stated that she was afraid. She also said that she "refused to marry a servant." Brier believes that the servant she referred to was Aye, who wanted to marry her in order to establish his own claim to the throne.

The Hittite king did send one of his sons to marry Ankhesenamen, but the young prince was murdered on the way at the order of Egypt's highest general, Horemheb. The evidence suggests that poor Ankhesenamen ended up marrying Aye anyway. What happened to her next is not known. However, Aye did became pharaoh of Egypt. After his death he was succeeded as pharaoh by Horemheb, who did his best to erase the memories of Tutankhamen and Aye from history. He was so successful that very little was known of Tutankhamen until the rediscovery of the boy king's almost perfectly intact tomb in 1922.

Weird News Stories

BACON BINARY

Francis Bacon was the father of the modern computer: in 1605 he developed a cipher using only *a* and *b* in five letter combinations, each representing a letter of the alphabet, demonstrating that only two signs are required to transmit information. Towards the end of the century, Leibniz developed the principle into the binary system that is the basis of modern computers. 0 and 1 can be combined to express any number.

The Story of King Zog 1865–1961

On Saturday 1 September 1928 Europe gained a new kingdom and its only Muslim king. His name? Zog I of the Albanians, a thirty-two-year-old Muslim man. Few foreign journalists were present in the Parliament House in Tirana to hear him swear his oath on the Koran and the Bible, yet the birth of the Kingdom of Albania did not go unnoticed abroad. King Zog became an international curiosity. He is noted as the most atypical European monarch of the twentieth century, a man entirely without royal connections who created his own kingdom. By contemporaries, he was variously labeled "the last ruler of romance," "an appalling gangster," "the modern Napoleon," "the finest patriot," and "frankly a cad." Even today his reputation is disputed, but Zog is undeniably one of the foremost figures in Albanian history. Though notorious for cut-throat political intrigue, he promised to bring order and progress to a land that had long known little of either. "It was I who made Albania," he claimed.

Zog's reign ended in 1939 when Italian Fascists forced him into exile, and post-war Stalinists kept him there despite his best efforts to return. The *Times* described him as "the bizarre King Zog" and portrayed him as the product of a unique time and place. He was well known as a man who who fired back at assassins and paid his bills with gold bullion, quite the opposite of any modern European monarch.

Grisly Tales from History

Trial by Combat

Middle Ages

In medieval times, if the court couldn't sort out a quarrel between two people, the judge would allow what was called "Trial by Combat". This meant that the two arguing parties would arm themselves with a sword or axe and fight to the death. Sometimes they simply killed each other but if one survived, then he was deemed to have won the argument.

William the Conqueror circa 1027–1087

King William I of England, better known as William the Conqueror, was born of a liaison between the devilish Duke Robert I of Normandy and a tanner's daughter named Herleve or Herleva and popularly remembered as Arlette or Arletta.

When William was about eight, his father decided to go on a pilgrimage to Jerusalem. Before leaving, Robert called his vassals together and ordered them to swear fealty to William. Reluctantly, the men obeyed. Perhaps Robert did not expect to return from the Holy Land; if so, he was right. He died on his journey, and his illegitimate son became the new Duke of Normandy.

When William was in his early twenties he married the daughter of Count Baldwin V of Flanders, Matilda. In 1051

William paid a visit to his cousin, the King of England, Edward the Confessor. Although he had a young wife, Edward was celibate and therefore childless. So he promised to make William his heir (or at least, that's what William claimed). However, in January of 1066 the dying King Edward named Harold as his successor, making William furious. It was not long before William had his revenge. In September of 1066 he invaded England, and on 14 October he defeated Harold at the Battle of Hastings. Famously, Harold was killed by an arrow through the eye, and so William became England's king, his coronation taking place on Christmas Day.

The conqueror ruthlessly put down all opponents and subjugated the English people. William's family life was often turbulent and at various times he actually fought against his eldest son Robert for the crown of Normandy. However, the King and Robert were later reconciled, and, when William died, he left Normandy to Robert. William Rufus inherited the throne of England.

William was still frequenting battlefields in his early sixties. While fighting the French at the Battle of Mantes, he was thrown against the pommel of his saddle so violently that his intestines burst. Five weeks later, on 9 September 1087, England's conqueror died. His servants stripped him bare and abandoned his body, but a kind-hearted knight arranged a funeral for him at the abbey of St Stephen in Caen. The funeral was disrupted by the outbreak of a fire. After extinguishing it, the pallbearers tried to cram the king's bloated corpse into a sarcophagus which was too small. The body exploded, creating a horrible smell that sent mourners running for the exits. Over the ensuing centuries William's tomb was twice desecrated by French rebels, an ignoble end for one of history's greatest conquerors.

60

? ! ? ! ? ! ? ! ? ! ? ! ? ! ?

The Female Pharaoh
Ancient Egypt

The civilization of Ancient Egypt lasted for more than 3,000 years and made Egypt one of the richest countries in the world. The people were ruled by Pharaohs who were believed to be descendants of God and if they didn't obey them then bad fortune would befall them. There was once a female Pharaoh called Hatshepsut who is always depicted in Ancient Egyptian drawings as wearing men's clothes because a woman wasn't really allowed to be Pharaoh but she happened to be the only child of the previous Pharaoh able to take up the job!

? ! ? ! ? ! ? ! ? ! ? ! ? ! ?

St Wenceslas, Duke of Bohemia ("Good King Wenceslas")
AD 907–935

Good King Wenceslas looked out, on the Feast of Stephen,
When the snow lay round about, deep and crisp and even.
Brightly shone the moon that night, though the frost was cruel,
When a poor man came in sight, gathering winter fuel.

You are probably familiar with the Christmas carol about Good King Wenceslas. But did you know that Wenceslas was a real person? He was born into the royal Premysl dynasty of Bohemia (located in what is now the Czech Republic).

According to legend, the original Premysl was a plowman who married a Bohemian princess named Libussa during the eighth century. Their descendants eventually united the warring tribes of Bohemia into one duchy. The first known Premysl ruler was Wenceslas's grandfather, Duke Borivoy I, who made Prague Castle the family seat. Wenceslas was born around 907 in the castle of Stochov near Prague. The castle is gone now, but there is still an oak tree there that was supposedly planted by Ludmila when Wenceslas was born. His nannies watered the tree with his bath water, which supposedly made the tree strong. The church Wenceslas attended also exists today.

At the age of eighteen he began to rule for himself. A stern but fair monarch, he stopped the persecution of priests and tamed the rebellious nobility. He was known for his kindness to the poor, as depicted in later verses of the carol. He was especially charitable to children, helping young orphans and slaves.

Many of the Bohemian nobles resented Wenceslas's attempts to spread Christianity, and were displeased when he swore allegiance to the king of Germany, Henry I. The duke's most deadly enemy proved to be his own brother, Boleslav, who joined the nobles who were plotting his brother's assassination. He invited Wenceslas to a religious festival and then attacked him on his way to mass. As the two were struggling, Boleslav's supporters jumped in and murdered Wenceslas. "Good King" Wenceslas died on 20 September 929. He was in his early twenties and had ruled Bohemia for five years. Today he is remembered as the patron saint of the Czech Republic.

A MAMMOTH TALE

From the 1660 report of Captain William Taylor, Master, *British Banner:*

"On the 25th of April, in lat. 12 deg. 7 min. 8 sec., and long. 93 deg. 52 min. E., with the sun over the main-yard, felt a strong sensation as if the ship was trembling. Sent the second mate aloft to see what was up. The latter called out to me to go up the fore rigging and look over the bows. I did so, and saw an enormous serpent shaking the bowsprit with a second animal, and a trampling of the tracks, as if the two creatures had been excited by the meeting. Then the two went on together.

"The hunter followed. Suddenly, one afternoon, he saw them. They were enormous hairy elephants with great white tusks curved upward. The hair was a dark chestnut color, very heavy on the hindquarters, but lighter toward the front. The beasts moved very slowly."

The last of the mammoths are believed to have died more than 12,000 years ago, and the hunter knew nothing about them. But did he see mammoths?

King Louis XIV 17th Century

When King Louis was in his teens he fell in love with Marie
Mancini, a niece of Cardinal Mazarin. The two secretly became
engaged, but Louis's mother refused to allow the match. Marie
Mancini was packed off to Italy to marry a nobleman, and Louis
reluctantly agreed to a political marriage with Maria Theresa,
the daughter of the king of Spain. The couple would have seven
children, but only one, a son named Louis, survived to
adulthood.

In 1661, when Louis XIV was twenty-two years old, he
became the sole ruler of France. He was an absolute monarch, as
expressed in the famous quote attributed to him, "L'etat c'est
moi" ("I am the state"). Identifying himself with Apollo, the
Greek god of the sun, Louis XIV came to be called "the Sun
King," as his court revolved around him like planets around the
sun. Louis is perhaps best remembered as the king who built
Versailles.

Every aspect of the king's life was conducted with pomp and
ceremony. He was awakened each morning at eight by his First
Valet de Chambre, who slept on a folding bed in the king's
room. Then the First Physician, the First Surgeon, and Louis's
former nanny entered the room to check the king's health.
Fifteen minutes later the Grand Chamberlain and other favoured
courtiers were admitted to watch the king dress. The valet
always handed the royal shirt to the most important courtier in
the room, who had the honour of handing it to Louis.

Louis XIV also succeeded in establishing and increasing the
influence and central authority of the King of France at the
expense of the Church and the nobles. Louis sought to reinforce
traditional Gallicanism, a doctrine limiting the authority of the
Pope in France. He convened an assembly of clergymen
(*Assemblée du Clergé*) in November 1681. Before it was

dissolved in June 1682, it had agreed to the *Declaration of the Clergy of France*. The power of the King of France was increased in contrast to the power of the Pope, which was reduced. The Pope was not allowed to send papal legates to France without the king's consent.

Such legates as could enter France, furthermore, required further approval before they could exercise their power. Bishops were not to leave France without royal approval; no government officials could be excommunicated for acts committed in pursuance of their duties; and no appeal could be made to the Pope without the approval of the king. The king was allowed to enact ecclesiastical laws, and all regulations made by the Pope were deemed invalid in France without the assent of the monarch.

Louis revoked the *Edict of Nantes* in 1685. The edict had given French Protestants the right to worship as they chose, after the revocation thousands of Huguenots (Protestants) fled the country, which seriously weakened France's economy. Europe's protestant rulers turned against Louis and war ensued.

The final years of Louis XIV's reign were marred by his persecution of Protestants and bitter losses in war. Louis himself died an agonizing death from gangrene on 1 September 1715. He was succeeded by his great-grandson, King Louis XV.

NO DRUMMING

The magistrate of Tedworth in Wiltshire, England, could not have imagined the consequences when he confiscated the drum belonging to William Drury – an itinerant musician caught in some shady dealings – and told him to leave the district.

That was in March 1662. Hardly had the culprit left Tedworth when the drum began to produce drumming noises itself. It also flew around Magistrate Mompesson's house, seen by several people besides the magistrate.

After several sleepless nights, he had the drum broken into pieces. Still the drumming continued. Nor was that all. Shoes flew through the air, and chamber pots were emptied onto beds. Children were levitated. A horse's rear leg was forced into its mouth.

The possibility that the exiled drummer had sneaked back and was causing the trouble was fairly well ruled out when it was discovered that he had been arrested for theft in the city of Gloucester and sent to the colonies. The Reverend Joseph Glanville, chaplain to King Charles II, came to Tedworth to investigate the phenomena. He heard the drumming himself, and collected eyewitness reports from the residents. No natural cause was found for the effects, which stopped exactly one year after they had started.

The Barbarian Kings 4th–5th Century AD

The Franks were a group of Germanic tribes who shared similar laws and customs. In the fourth and fifth centuries AD, they began settling in the Roman region of Gaul (which included what is now Belgium, France, Luxembourg, and some of Germany and Italy). At first they lived in Belgium, but eventually most of Gaul would belong to the Frankish Empire.

The Franks were allies of Rome, and King Merovech of the Franks is said to have fought with the Romans against Attila the Hun. Merovech's son, Childeric I was said to be excessively wanton, and being King of the Franks he began to dishonour their daughters." For this bad behaviour, Childeric's subjects drove him out of his kingdom. He went into hiding at the court of King and Queen Basina of Thuringia in Germany.

After eight years, Childeric's subjects accepted him back as their king. But it seems Childeric hadn't changed his womanizing ways during his stay in Thuringia. After he left, Queen Basina missed him so much that she followed him back to his kingdom. When Childeric asked why she had traveled so far to see him, she said, "I know your worth, and that you are very strong, and therefore I have come to live with you." Childeric married her, and she gave birth to his son and successor, King Clovis I.

Grisly Tales from History

No One Under Thirty

The Aztecs

The Aztecs lived in Mexico from around AD 1345 to AD 1520. They had some very strict rules.
Alcohol was banned unless you were over thirty years old and even then you had to be ill to drink it. If someone did something considered wrong, the King would have them knocked down, and, if they committed a second crime, they were killed. They had funny superstitions, too. If a warrior was feeling a bit uncertain about a battle he had to dig up the body of a woman who had died in childbirth. He was then supposed to cut off her hair and fingers and stick them onto his shield. It was supposed to bring him luck.

King Clovis and Queen Clotilda circa AD 292

Son of King Childeric 1, King Clovis conquered most of Gaul, ruthlessly murdering relatives who stood in his way, and united the Franks under his rule. He made Paris the capital of his empire, setting the stage for the future French monarchy. In fact, France is named after the Franks. In 492 or 493 Clovis married a princess named Clotilda, the niece of King Gundobad of Burgundy. Like most of the Franks, Clotilda was a Catholic. Clovis allowed her to have their children baptized, but she was unable to convert her pagan husband.

In 496, during a ferocious battle with another Germanic tribe, the Alemanni, Clovis prayed to Clotilda's god, promising to convert to Catholicism if he won. He did win and, according to traditional accounts, was baptized on Christmas Day along with 3,000 of his soldiers, and became a champion of Catholicism.

After her husband's death in 511, Queen Clotilda spent her life caring for the poor. She is remembered as a Catholic saint, St Clotilda, and her feast is traditionally celebrated on 3 June.

Weird News Stories

SOMNIUM

The first piece of science fiction was Kepler's story "Somnium", published after his death in 1630. Cyrano de Bergerac's *Voyage to the Moon* (published 1657), often cited as the first work of science fiction, is not only later, but fails to qualify because it is political satire rather than science fiction.

69

? ! ? ! ? ! ? ! ? ! ? ! ? ! ?

FASCINATING FACTS

Egyptian Cats

Ancient Egypt

In Egyptian mythology, Bastet (also spelled Bast, Ubasti, and Pasht) was an ancient goddess, worshipped at least since the Second Dynasty, from around 2575 BC. Originally she was viewed as the protector goddess of Lower Egypt, and consequently depicted as a fierce lion. Indeed, her name means (female) devourer. As a protector, she was seen as defender of the pharaoh, and consequently of the chief god, Ra. Bastet was originally a goddess of the sun, but later changed by the Greeks to a goddess of the moon. In Greek mythology, Bast is also known as *Aelurus* (Greek for *cat*).

By the Middle Kingdom (roughly between 2030 BC and 1640 BC), she was generally regarded as a domestic cat rather than a lioness. Occasionally, however, she was depicted holding a lioness mask, which hinted at suppressed ferocity. Because domestic cats tend to be tender and protective toward their offspring, Bast was also regarded as a good mother, and she was sometimes depicted with numerous kittens. Consequently, a woman who wanted children sometimes wore an amulet showing the goddess with kittens, the number of which indicated her own desired number of children. Due to the threat to the food supply caused by vermin such as mice and rats, cats in Egypt were revered, sometimes being given golden jewellery to wear, and being allowed to eat from the same plates as their owners. They were also prized for their ability to fight and kill snakes, especially cobras. Consequently, as the main cat (rather than lion) deity, Bast was revered as the patron of cats, and thus it was in the temple at Per-Bast that dead (and mummified) cats were brought for burial. Over 300,000 mummified cats were discovered when Bast's temple at Per-Bast was excavated.

? ! ? ! ? ! ? ! ? ! ? ! ? ! ?

St Patrick and the Irish Kings circa AD 390

In his youth Saint Patrick (originally named Maewyn) spent six years as a shepherd, caring for his master's flock under harsh conditions. It was during this lonely, desperate time that he learned to pray deeply. "More and more did the love of God, and my fear of him and faith increase," he later wrote.

When Maewyn was in his early twenties he dreamt that he heard a voice telling him to leave Ireland, saying, "Lo, your ship is ready." Knowing that it was a vision from God, Maewyn set off on his journey. After a journey of 200 miles he found a ship that was about to set sail from Ireland. He begged to be given passage but was turned away. Maewyn began to pray. Suddenly the crew called him back, they had changed their minds, and Maewyn was allowed on board. Following a mystical experience in which he heard the voice of the Irish begging him to return, he decided to become a priest, despite the objections of his family. It was perhaps at this point that he took the name Patrick (Patricius Magonus Sucatus). He felt that God was calling him back to Ireland, but it was some time before he received the church's permission to go.

Apparently Patrick decided that his mission to convert the people of Ireland would be easier if he received the blessing of the high king, Laoghaire (the son of Niall of the Nine Hostages). He chose a very bold way of getting Laoghaire's attention. Each year the Irish people celebrated a druid festival in which bonfires were lit on hilltops throughout the country. No fire was supposed to be lit until the high king had kindled his fire on the sacred hill of Tara, but Patrick violated this rule by building a huge Easter bonfire on the Hill of Slane, a few miles from Tara. When Laoghaire saw the distant flames, he angrily called his warriors together and went to confront Patrick.

Patrick turned an enemy into a friend. He impressed Laoghaire,

and the king invited him to Tara. There the king's druids mocked Patrick, asking him if he could make it snow. According to legend, Patrick replied that only God could make it snow, and at that moment it began to snow. When Patrick crossed himself, the snow stopped. Awed, the high king gave Patrick permission to continue his missionary work. Laoghaire himself never converted to Christianity, but his wife, daughters, and brother did.

For some thirty years Patrick travelled tirelessly throughout Ireland, spreading his Christian message. Patrick established hundreds of churches, and is credited with single-handedly converting the vast majority of the Irish people to Christianity. When he died around 461, the whole country mourned. Today he is honoured as Ireland's patron saint.

Grisly Tales from History
Slaves to the Pope
15th Century

Pope Innocent VIII, 1432–1492, famed for his worldliness, once received a gift of 100 matching items. The kind pope generously distributed them as gratuities to various cardinals and friends. The items were actually Moorish slaves. It was Innocent who later appointed the Spanish Dominican friar Tomás de Torquemada to serve as the grand inquisitor (in 1487) under whose authority thousands of Jews, suspected witches, and miscellaneous heretics were killed or tortured during the Spanish Inquisition.

King Ludwig II 1845–86

In 1886, King Ludwig II (also known as the Swan King, the Mad King of Bavaria, the Dream King, and Mad Ludwig) was officially declared insane by the government and incapable of executing his governmental powers, and his uncle, Prince Luitpold, was declared regent. The psychiatrist Professor Bernhard von Gudden, despite never having examined Ludwig, declared Ludwig to be suffering from paranoia (comparable to a modern diagnosis of paranoid schizophrenia). Their chief evidence was stories of Ludwig's odd behaviour, collected from palace servants by his political enemies. As many of these stories were not first-hand accounts and may have been obtained with bribery or threats, their reliability is highly questionable. Many historians believe that Ludwig was sane, an innocent victim of political intrigue. Others believe he may have suffered from a substance-abuse problem in an effort to control chronic toothache rather than mental illness.

The relatives of Bavarian King Ludwig II have long been resigned to the fact that they have a colourful legacy to look back on, but a modern descendant of the king's stable master doesn't want anyone to pass that legacy on to one of his ancestors. In fact, he was so desperate that he actually took the case to court in 2005. Part of this court case was to decide once and for all whether Ludwig II was gay or not.

King Ludwig II (1845–86), remembered as a good-looking man whose subjects had a deep respect for him, was known to keep a diary that noted down his difficulties in reconciling his Catholic faith and his sexual desires. It has long been speculated that he enjoyed "overly friendly" relationships with his male servants, especially, it is rumoured, the head of the stables. The relationship even made its way into a song alluding to a homosexual relation-ship between the Ludwig and the stable master.

Although the king's sexual preference remains open to debate, it is known that he postponed his wedding numerous times before canceling it altogether. In 2005, the stable master's great-grandson Michael Siegfried Graf von Holnstein is very upset at the thought of anyone calling his father's father's father gay.

"It injures his reputation and is an insult. I'm not going to let that happen," he said, according to Berlin's tabloid *BZ*. "If it remains uncontested, it could be seen as a confirmation."

Weird News Stories

PLUMPERS

In the eighteenth century, many elegant gentlemen wore "plumpers" (cork pads) in their cheeks to disguise the hollows left by rotten teeth.

Attila and the Huns circa AD 370

The Huns arrived in southeastern Europe around 370 AD. The Roman historian Ammianus described them as wild, hideous barbarians who ate raw meat and did everything on horseback, even sleep. They were divided into independent groups called "hordes" which apparently had their own chieftains; it is generally believed that the Huns did not have a king at this time.

By 432 the Huns were united under a single king, named Rua,

and had taken over lands belonging to other German tribes before moving into the Eastern Roman Empire. When Rua died in 434, his brother's sons, Bleda and Attila, inherited his huge empire. They demanded additional tribute from the Romans. The Romans agreed, but apparently didn't pay all they had promised, so Attila attacked them, destroying city after city.

However, at least one Roman woman saw Attila as a potential hero. Her name was Honoria, and she was the sister of the Western Roman emperor, Valentinian III. She had been sent into exile for having an affair with an officer of her household. Trapped in a convent and desperate to escape, she sent Attila her ring and a plea for help. So Attila informed the Romans that he intended to marry Honoria but in return he expected to be given half the Western Roman empire as her dowry. The Romans refused Attila's demands, and Attila went on the attack. He invaded Gaul, but the Romans defeated him in battle for the first time. Attila then withdrew from Gaul, although he got his revenge by destroying a number of Italian cities. After Honoria's overtures to Attila were discovered, Valentinian forced her to marry a Roman senator. No one knows what happened to her after that.

However, Attila had plenty of wives, and in 453, while plotting another invasion of the Eastern Roman empire, he took some time off to get married again. His bride was a beautiful girl named Ildico, and their wedding night was the last night of Attila's life. Late the next morning, his servants broke in and found Attila dead, with Ildico weeping nearby. The drunken Attila had suffered a terrible nosebleed in the night and choked to death on his own blood.

But did Attila really die of natural causes? Many historians believe Attila was murdered, most probably poisoned. The Huns did not last long without their great king. Attila's empire was divided among his numerous sons, who immediately started fighting each other. Their oppressed subjects took this opportunity to rebel against Hun rule. Within a few years, the empire fell apart and the Huns all but disappeared from history. By the seventh century, they had disappeared from history.

Weird News Stories

FATHERS AND SONS

On 13 February 1746, a Frenchman named Jean Marie Dunbarry was hanged for murdering his father. Precisely a century later, on 13 February 1846, another Jean Marie Dunbarry, great-grandson of the other, was also hanged for murdering his father.

Dutch Royalty Late 17th Century

Did you know that women have held the throne in the Netherlands since 1890, when Queen Wilhelmina inherited the throne at the age of ten? Her mother, Emma of Waldeck–Pyrmont, served as regent until Wilhelmina turned eighteen. Wilhelmina is known to have helped her country remain neutral during World War I. When the Nazis invaded the

Netherlands in 1940, the Queen escaped to England from where she brought hope to her occupied nation through regular radio broadcasts.

In 1945, the queen returned home and abdicated three years later in favour of her daughter Juliana. Queen Juliana reigned until 1980, when she too abdicated in favour of her eldest daughter, Beatrix. Queen Beatrix continues to reign today. Her mother, who was called Princess Juliana after her abdication, died in 2004 at the age of ninety-four.

Anastasia Romanov and the legend of Anne Anderson
20th Century

Grand Duchess Anastasia Nicholaevna was born on 18 June 1901. Her parents were Nicholas II, the last Tsar of Russia, and his wife Alexandra. Anastasia had three elder sisters: Olga, Tatiana, and Maria. Her only brother, Alexei (often translated as "Alexis") was born in 1904. For years Russia had been in upheaval. On March 15, 1917 Tsar Nicholas was forced to abdicate. At the time of the abdication Anastasia and her siblings were suffering from measles. While they were confined to their beds the palace was taken over by soldiers. The imperial family was now prisoners.

The family were moved and held captive at Ipatiev House in Ekaterinburg, Siberia, for seventy-eight days. Their last day was 16 July 1918. Late that night, the family was awakened and told to get dressed. After midnight they were taken to the cellar where, believing they were to be photographed, they stood in two rows. Anastasia, carrying her dog Jemmy, stood with her sisters, their doctor, and three servants. Suddenly armed men burst into the room and began firing. Apparently, Anastasia was seen huddled against the wall, covering her head with her arms. Eventually Tatiana and Maria died. A maid who did not die from the gunshots was bayoneted. By some accounts, Anastasia was also bayoneted many times.

However, there is much confusion about how Anastasia died. Some people refuse to believe that she died at all. On the night of 17 February 1920, less than two years after the murders in Ipatiev House, a woman jumped off a bridge in Berlin. She was rescued and taken to a hospital. With no ID and refusing to give her identity, she was sent to a mental asylum. Legend has it that when she was given a list of the tsar's daughters' names, she crossed out all except Anastasia. When one of Alexandra's ladies-in-waiting visited her, the woman hid beneath a blanket. The lady-in-waiting called her an imposter and stormed off. She eventually insisted on being called Anna Anderson. Many people believed the woman's tale, and after her release in 1922 she lived on the charity of various sympathizers.

Eventually she explained her escape from the imperial family's assassins. She had been bayoneted, she said, but survived because the soldiers' weapons were blunt. After the murders a soldier named Tschaikovsky saw that she was still moving and rescued her. She said she had come to Berlin to seek out her aunt, Princess Irene. Princess Irene did meet the woman eventually and denied that she resembled Anastasia. Yet Irene is said to have later cried about the meeting and admitted, "She is similar, she is similar." Irene's son Prince Sigismund, a childhood friend of Anastasia, sent the woman a list of questions. Her answers convinced him that she was Anastasia.

Her detractors pointed out that she never spoke Russian. However, when she was addressed in Russian she understood and answered in other languages. She said she wouldn't speak Russian because it was the language spoken by those who had killed her family. She spoke good English, German and French – which would have been unusual for someone not born into

nobility at the time. She had scars that she said came from being
shot and bayoneted. Anderson and Anastasia had other physical
similarities. Anderson had a foot deformity like Anastasia's.
Anthropologists who studied their photographs found their faces
to be very similar. One famous anthropologist, Dr Otto Reche,
testified in court that Anastasia and Anna Anderson had to be
either the same person or identical twins.

Anderson brought a suit in a German court in 1938 to prove
her identity and claim part of the inheritance. The case dragged
on until 1970. Reche's testimony, made after examining
photographs of Anastasia and Anna Anderson, came in 1964. A
handwriting expert, who was not paid for her testimony, also
swore that Anderson was Anastasia. Finally the court ruled, not
that Anderson wasn't Anastasia, but that she hadn't proved it.
The remains of the imperial family were exhumed in 1991.
Portions of nine skeletons were found, and DNA testing
confirmed they included Nicholas, Alexandra, and three of their
daughters. Two bodies remain missing. The consensus is that
they are those of Alexei and one of his sisters, possibly
Anastasia. Recent DNA analysis of hair and tissue samples from
Anderson seemed to prove that she was not Anastasia, although
many still claim that she was.

? ! ? ! ? ! ? ! ? ! ? ! ? ! ?

Tales of Troy
Ancient Greece

According to mythology, around 1250 BC the Trojan War started and was to last for ten years. Apparently Helen of Sparta was so beautiful that all the Greek kings wanted to marry her. She eventually married Menelaus but then fell in love with Paris of Troy and went to live with him in the walled city leaving her husband behind. Her ex-husbands brother was so angry at what she'd done to his brother that he and the Greek army tried for ten years to get into the walled city to get her back without much luck. Eventually they came up with the idea of the now famous wooden horse. The Trojans found the wooden horse outside their gates one day and wheeled it inside. The horse was full of soldiers who leapt out after dark to open the city gates to let in the rest of the army. They attacked the sleeping city, killing all the men and making the women and children into slaves. Although the Greek poet Homer wrote the story, a German explorer in the nineteenth century believed it to be true and set out to find Troy. He is said to have found the remains of a city which might be Troy in what is now Turkey!

? ! ? ! ? ! ? ! ? ! ? ! ? ! ?

┌───┐
│ Weird News Stories   │
│ # GOLD FEVER   │
│   │
│    │
│   │
│ The US Mint once printed a run   │
│ of gold coins bearing the   │
│ erroneous inscription: "In Gold   │
│ We Trust."   │
└───┘

Princess Diana 1961–1997

Diana Frances Spencer was born on 1 July 1961 at Park House, the home her parents rented on the royal family's estate at Sandringham. As a child she occasionally played with Prince Andrew and Prince Edward, who were close to her in age. Diana had two older sisters, Sarah and Jane, and a younger brother, Charles.

Her romance with the Prince of Wales began in 1980. The oldest child of British monarch Queen Elizabeth II, he was twelve years older than Diana, and had previously dated her sister, Sarah. Almost from the start, the press took a special interest in "Lady Di." They staked out her apartment and followed her everywhere. Diana later said that she found the constant attention unbearable.

Diana and Charles were married 29 July 1981 at St Paul's

Cathedral. The wedding was broadcast in seventy-four countries and watched by 750 million people worldwide. Diana was the first English woman to marry an heir to the throne in over 300 years. At the ceremony the Archbishop of Canterbury said, "Here is the stuff of which fairy tales are made." But the fairy tale was an illusion, as Diana had already discovered. Prince Charles was still in love with an old girlfriend, Camilla Parker-Bowles. Distraught, Diana is rumored to have developed bulimia and attempted suicide. Despite her problems, she was a devoted mother to her two sons, Prince William and Prince Harry. She worked tirelessly for charity, and was loved by the public for her warmth and humanity.

"There were three of us in this marriage, so it was a bit crowded," Princess Diana remarked years later. In 1992, Princess Diana decided to expose the truth about her relationship with Prince Charles to the public. She secretly collaborated with author Andrew Morton on his book *Diana, Her True Story*. The princess's direct involvement in the writing of the book was not revealed to the public until after her death.

The separation of the Prince and Princess of Wales was announced on 9 December 1992 and the divorce became official on 28 August 1996. Princess Diana kept the title Princess of Wales and continued to work for her favorite charities. She and Prince Charles had joint custody of their sons.

In 1997 Princess Diana began a love affair with Emad "Dodi" Al-Fayed, the son of billionaire businessman Mohammed Al-Fayed. Their romance ended abruptly on 31 August 1997 when both were killed in a car accident in Paris while fleeing from paparazzi. Princess Diana's sudden death led to an unprecedented worldwide outpouring of grief and love. As her brother said at her funeral, she was "the unique, the complex, the extraordinary and irreplacable Diana, whose beauty, both internal and external, will never be extinguished from our minds." In 2006 an inquest into her death was requested by Mohammed Al-Fayed and granted. The inquest is to be attended by a jury, unprecedented in British Royal history. Many believe that her death was not an accident but that she was deliberately murdered by the British Secret Service in order to prevent her from marrying into the Al-Fayed family.

Weird News Stories

BESTSELLER

The first "bestselling" novel was Samuel Richardson's *Pamela, or Virtue Rewarded* (1740), which went into edition after edition, and was translated into most European languages. Rousseau's *La Nouvelle Heloise* (1760) surpassed it; it was so popular that lending libraries would lend it out by the hour. The first American bestseller was *Charlotte Temple* (1791) by an Englishwoman, Susanna Haswell Rowson, a melodramatic and badly written book that nevertheless went through 200 editions.

Did Joan of Arc Return from the Dead?

On 30 May 1431 Joan of Arc was burnt as a heretic by the English; she was only nineteen years old. She regarded herself as a messenger from Heaven, sent to save the French from their enemies the English (who were in league with the Burgundians who captured her). At the age of thirteen Joan began to hear voices, which she later identified as those of St Gabriel, St Michael, St Marguerite and St Catherine.

When the news of the encirclement of Orleans reached her little village in Lorraine, Domremy, her voices told her to go to lift the siege. Her military career was brief but spectacular: in a year she won many remarkable victories, and saw Charles VII crowned at Rheims. Then she was captured by the Burgundians, sold to the English for ten thousand francs, tried as a witch, and burnt alive. But that, oddly enough, was not quite the end of "the Maid".

"One month after Paris had returned to her allegiance to King Charles," writes Anatole France, "a women appeared in Lorraine. She was about twenty-five years old and made herself known to people as Jeanne the Maid." This was in May 1436, five years after Joan had died at the stake. It sounds very obviously as if some impostor had decided to pose as Joan the Maid. But there is some astonishing evidence that suggests that this is not so. Joan's two younger brothers, Petit-Jean and Pierre, were still serving in the army, and they had no doubt whatever that their sister had been burnt at Rouen.

So when they heard that a woman claiming to be Joan was at Metz, and that she had expressed a wish to meet them, the brothers hastened to Metz – Petit-Jean was not far away, being the provost of Vaucouleurs. One chronicler describes how the brothers went to the village of La-Grange-aux-Ormes, two and a half miles south of Metz, where a tournament was being held. A knight in armour was galloping around an obstacle course and pulling stakes expertly out of the ground; this was the person who claimed to be their sister. The brothers rode out on to the field, prepared to challenge the impostor. But when Petit-Jean demanded, "Who are you? The "impostor" raised her visor, and both brothers gasped in astonishment as they recognized their sister Joan.

The next day her brothers took her to Vaucouleurs, where she spent a week, apparently accepted by many people who had seen her there seven years earlier. After this she spent three weeks at a small town called Marville, then went on a pilgrimage to see the Black Virgin called Notre Dame de Liance, between Laon and Rheims. Then she went to stay with Elizabeth, Duchess of Luxembourg, at Arlon. Meanwhile her brother Petit-Jean went to see the king and announced that his sister Joan was still alive. We do not know the king's reaction, but he ordered his treasurer to give Petit-Jean a hundred francs. An entry in the treasury accounts of Orleans for 9 August 1436, states that the council authorized payment of a courier who had brought letters from "Jeanne la Pucelle" (Joan the Maid).

The records of these events are to be found in the basic standard work on Joan of Arc, Jules Quicherat's five-volume *Trial and Rehabilitation of Joan of Arc* (1841), which contains all the original documents. One of these documents states that on 24 June 1437 Joan's miraculous powers returned to her.

In 1440, according to the journal "of a Bourgeois of Paris", Joan was arrested, tried and publicly exhibited as a malefactor. A sermon was preached against her, and she was forced to confess publicly that she was an impostor. Her story, according to the "Bourgeois of Paris", was that she had gone to Rome about 1433 to seek absolution for striking her mother. She had, she said, engaged as a soldier in war in the service of the Holy

Father Eugenius, and worn man's apparel. This, presumably, gave her the idea of pretending to be the Maid . . .

But the whole of this story is doubtful in the extreme. To begin with, Joan then returned to Metz, and continued to be accepted as "la Pucelle". In 1443 her brother Pierre refers to her in a petition as "Jeanne la Pucelle, my sister", and her cousin Henry de Voulton mentions that Petit-Jean, Pierre and their sister la Pucelle used to visit the village of Sermaise and feast with relations, all of whom accepted her. Fourteen years later she makes an appearance in the town of Saumur, and is again accepted by the officials of the town as the Maid. And after that she vanishes from history, presumably living out the rest of her life quietly with her husband in Metz.

As far as we know, The Dame des Armoires never explained how she came to escape the flames. But then presumably she would not know the answer to this question. She would only know that she had been rescued, and that someone else had died in her place – perhaps another "witch". It is easy to see how this could have come about. We know that Joan was an extraordinarily persuasive young lady, and that dozens of people, from Robert de Baudricourt to the Dauphin, who began by assuming she was mad, ended by believing that she was being guided by divine voices. We know that even in court Joan declared that she could hear St Catherine telling her what to say. Even at her trial she had certain friends; a priest called Loyseleur was her adviser, and the Earl of Wessex remained close.

It would not be at all surprising if there had been a successful plot to rescue her. And it is possible that the English themselves may have been involved in such a plot; when Joan was apparently burnt at the stake in Rouen the crowd was kept at a distance by eight hundred English soldiers, which would obviously prevent anyone coming close enough to recognize her. At the trial for her rehabilitation in 1456 the executioner's evidence was entirely second-hand, although three of Joan's comrades who were with her at the "end" – Ladvenu, Massieu and Isambard – were actually present. *If* Joan had been rescued, presumably they had also been involved in the plot.

The rehabilitation itself has its farcical aspects. It began in 1450, and Joan's mother was the person who set it in motion, supported by Joan's brother Pierre. We do not know whether Joan's mother accepted the Dame des Armoires as her daughter, but there can be no doubt that she lent credence to the claim by not denouncing her as an impostor. Yet now, she and Pierre joined in the claim that was based on the assertion that Joan was executed by the English in 1431. But then the aim of the rehabilitation was financial; Joan had been a rich woman, thanks to the generosity of the king, and the wealth remained frozen while Joan was excommunicated. So, whether or not Joan's family believed that the Dame des Armoires was the Maid, they now had good reason to try to have her rehabilitated even if it meant swearing that she was dead. If the Dame des Armoires was genuine, she must have felt there was a certain irony in the situation. She had been an embarrassment to everyone during her first career as the saintly virgin warrior; now she was just as much an embarrassment as the heroine returned from the dead. It is thankless work being a saint.

MOTHER GOOSE

Mother Goose was a real person – the author of songs and jingles published in 1716. Her name was Elizabeth Foster, and she was born in 1665; she married Isaac Goose at the age of twenty-eight, and died in Boston – where her nursery rhymes were published – at the age of ninety-two.

Chapter Six

A Brief, Unreliable History of . . .
Stone-Age Man

Stone-Age Man

Everything you ever wanted to know about
the people who brought us rock painting,
pet dogs, and fur bikinis.

1

The Stone Age was the prehistoric period of mankind, in other
words, what we did before we started writing a diary. It was
named after the most common murder instrument of the period,
a big, pointy rock.

2

The Old Stone Age started about a million years ago. Once a
certain breed of monkey decided that two legs were better than
four and started walking to work in the morning, he also realized
that he could use the spare hands to use tools and to throw a
stick. This also led on to man's first domesticated animal, the
dog, which liked to run after the sticks that Stone Age man
threw.

3

After the best part of a million years, man got tired of throwing
sticks for the dog to chase and started to want to eat some nicer
meals for a change. Also, his wife had been trying to persuade

him to settle down and build a house for half a million years or so, and he finally gave in. So the first farms were built, and man started to cultivate crops such as wheat and corn.

4

Stone-Age architecture left a lot to be desired. After a few hundred thousand years in caves, man started to try to build a house. One of the first attempts involved dragging some huge rocks a few hundred miles from Wales to Wiltshire in the UK, and then piling them up in a big circle. The Stonehenge housing project was generally regarded as a failure, due to omission of walls and roofs from the building plans.

5

While spending long winter nights in damp caves, man started to develop his artistic side by drawing paintings on the cave walls. Some believe that the surviving pictures of stick men and animals hold a deep message about the essential nature of mankind. Others believe that Stone Age man just wasn't very good at drawing.

6

Once man had cultivated grapes and grain, he quickly realized that he could turn them into alcohol. The first Stone Age drinking party in 50,000 BC went on for six months and only ended when a woolly mammoth trod on the vol au vents and a sabre-toothed tiger ate the musicians.

7

Stone Age fashion was fairly basic, as most kinds of material hadn't yet been invented. Fur and leather were the most common fabrics, as represented with total accuracy by Raquel Welch's bikini in *One Million Years BC*.

8

Pottery was first used in the Stone Age, as a container for food, drink and flowers. Metals such as copper were also used, just to confuse anyone who thought that the Stone Age was so-called because stone was the only material used for tools.

9

Stone Age man survived several ice ages although it is possible that the Neanderthal variety of man died out during a nasty cold snap about 25,000 years ago. The Neanderthals were smaller, uglier and hairier than modern humans, and it is thought that stories of the "little people" date from the time when they still co-existed with modern man.

10

The Stone Age ended at about three in the afternoon one December day 10,000 years ago, when the Bronze Age was officially declared open for business.

Future Bingo

The future history of the world is hard to predict. But as we look forward in fear and hope, why not have some fun while we're waiting?

Keep this **Future Bingo** sheet to hand, and cross off any events that actually happen in the future. If you get a full page of amazing future events, then shout out "House".

If you send the finished page to the **Future Bingo** corporation (at an address yet to be determined), you may even receive a mystery prize . . .

Flying saucers land on White House.	Rolling Stones admit they're too old to rock and roll.
United Nations declares war on Not So United Nations.	Presidential candidate admits truth, wins landslide.
Fresh fruit bad for you, admit doctors.	Las Vegas reopens as health spa.

Chapter Seven

Weird News: Christopher Columbus

Born in 1451 in the Italian port, of Genoa, Christopher Columbus was attracted to water. He went to sea as a pimpled youth, proceeded to marry the daughter of a Portuguese navigator and settled down happily in Lisbon.

Christopher was very highly influenced by his reading of a fashionable book of the period, Ptolemy's *Geography*. From this work Columbus learnt two main facts: firstly, that the world was a perfect sphere (which is clearly a mistake) and, secondly, that the known world extends in a continuous land-mass from the western extremities of Europe to the easternmost limit of Asia and that between the two ends of this landmass on the other side of the sphere, there was one single intervening ocean (which was clearly also a mistake). Theoretically, it would thus be possible, according to Ptolemy, to cross from Europe to Asia via the Atlantic Ocean. Ptolemy also reckoned that the proportions of land to ocean were identical and therefore the Atlantic would be too wide for any vessel in existence at the time to be able to cross. Columbus didn't like this part of the book so he dismissed it as incorrect.

On 3 August 1492, Columbus embarked from the port of Palos in his trusty boat the *Santa Maria* and set sail for a destination due west. On 12 October 1492, after quelling a potential mutiny on board by sheer force of personality, he landed in the Bahamas, believing himself to be in China. He kept notes on the native people, as if he were making notes about the Chinese, and he explored Haiti. He returned to Barcelona to a hero's welcome.

In September 1493, Columbus once again set sail, landing this time in Puerto Rico which he considered to be an island in the Indian Ocean. This is when things began to go badly wrong. A large number of colonizers had sailed with Columbus, thinking that they were about to get rich on gold. Columbus, however, was very keen that they should all plant vegetables. The unhappy Spaniards seized most of the boats and returned to Spain. Those who remained were disgusted to discover that the local food was horrible, the weather was lousy and there wasn't a nugget of gold to be found.

Columbus wasn't a man to be easily deterred by the big things in life. It was during his third voyage to the East Indies that Magellan and Da Gama actually did reach the Orient, thus discrediting Columbus completely while he was still claiming that Honduras was, in fact, Japan. Two years later, he returned to Spain, a broken man, but still pretty wealthy.

Weird News Stories

Weird News Stories

LOST AT SEA

Late in the eighteenth century a sailing ship off the coast of West Africa found itself becalmed in a placid ocean. The wind had dropped, and Jean-Magnus Dens, the Danish captain, ordered his crew to lower planks off the side from which they could scrape and clean the ship. Three men climbed onto the planks and began their work. They were scraping energetically when suddenly, out of the quiet sea around them, rose an immense octopus or squid. It seized two of the men and pulled them under the water. The third man leaped desperately into the rigging, but a gigantic arm pursued him, getting caught up in the shrouds. The sailor fainted from shock, and his horrified shipmates frantically hacked at the great tentacle, finally chopping it off. Meanwhile, five harpoons were being driven into the body of the beast in the forlorn hope of saving the two who had disappeared. The frightful struggle went on until, one by one, four of the lines broke. The men had to give up the attempt at killing the monster, which sank out of view. The unconscious. sailor, hanging limply in the shrouds, was gently taken down and placed in his bunk. He revived a little, but died in raving madness that night.

Countess of Blood

Countess Erzsébet Báthory (1560–1614), the Bloody Lady of Čachtice (Csejte), was a Hungarian countess who lived in Royal Hungary, in present-day Slovakia, a relative of the King of Poland and the Prince of Transylvania, Stefan Batory. She is considered the most infamous serial killer in Hungarian and Slovak history. She spent most of her life at the Čachtice Castle. After her husband's death, it is believed that Elizabeth Báthory tortured and killed an unknown number of young women, (though it is often cited as being in the hundreds), between the years 1585 and 1610. Although her husband and her relatives knew about her sadistic inclination, they did not directly intervene. After her husband's death any restraints he may have imposed on her (or she on herself) seemed completely removed. Her initial victims were local peasant girls, many of whom were lured to Čachtice by offers of well-paid work as maids in the castle. Later she may have begun to kill daughters of lower gentry, who were sent to her castle by their parents to learn high society etiquette by the opportunity to attend a sort of "finishing school". Abductions seem to have occurred as well. In 1611, she was imprisoned in Čachtice Castle, where she remained until her death three years later. Her nobility allowed her to avoid trial and execution, three of her four alleged collaborators were put to death.

Testimonies collected in 1610 and 1611 contain a total of over 300 witness accounts. Trial records include testimonies of the four persons indicted, as well as thirteen more witnesses. Priests, noblemen and commoners were questioned. Eye-witnesses included the castellan and other personnel of Báthory's Sárvár castle.

Some witnesses named relatives who had died while in Báthory's gynaeceum. Others reported having seen traces of torture on dead bodies, some of which were buried in graveyards, and others in unmarked locations.

The descriptions of torture that emerged during the trials were often based on hearsay. The atrocities described most consistently included: severe beatings over extended periods of time, often leading to death, burning, or mutilation of hands, sometimes also of faces and genitalia, biting the flesh off the faces, arms, and other bodily parts, freezing to death and the starving of victims.

According to the defendants, whose confessions were obtained under brutal torture, Báthory tortured and killed her victims not only at Čachtice, but also on her properties in Bécko, (Bratislava) and Vienna, and even en route between these locations.

In addition to the defendants, several people were named for supplying Báthory with young girls. The girls had been procured either by deception or by force.

104

Weird News Stories

WHEELS THAT FLY

Since 1760 seamen have recounted sightings of uniden- tified flying objects in the form of a wheel. The Persian Gulf sighting of 1906 was one of eleven recorded reports between 1848 and 1910. like most of the sea accounts of mysterious luminous wheels, this one remarked on the eery silence of the phenomenon. Also in common with most other such reports, nothing was said about humans or humanlike beings in the wheels, even though the ascent and descent of these objects were obviously controlled.

Were such glowing wheels in the sky an early and less sophisticated form of flying saucer? Were they operated by beings from other planets who kept themselves hidden or were invisible? Were they just visions of mariners too long at sea? No one has found an answer.

Chapter Eight

A Brief, Unreliable History of . . .
Ancient Civilizations

Ancient Civilizations

Everything you ever wanted to know about the people who invented writing, pyramids, human sacrifice and taxation.

1

One of the world's first great civilizations arose in the fourth millennium BC in the fertile valley between the Tigris and Euphrates rivers. Sumer was the first civilization to develop a writing system and thus can be said to mark the beginning of written history. The location of Sumer lies within the boundaries of modern-day Iraq.

2

After Sumer, the next great empires were the empire of Babylon (which arose in the same area) and Egypt. The Egyptians developed hieroglyphics to keep track of their many pharaohs and crop failures, but unfortunately all modern scholars have been able to decipher is that they were rather fond of eagles and cats.

3

Babylon was a truly great empire, responsible for such wonders of the ancient world as the Hanging Gardens of Babylon, and for literary works such as the *Epic of Gilgamesh*. Later on, Babylon got a weird reputation, largely because of a few narky references in the Bible, but at its height, Babylon was the epitome of civilization.

4

Some time around 3000 BC, there was a terrible flood in the Mediterranean or Middle Eastern region. We can be pretty sure of this because from Noah's Ark to the Babylonian flood myths, every culture of the region told stories of the great flood that came one day without warning.

5

The Chinese developed writing at more or less the same time as the Sumerians although they had already been using pictograms for a few millennia. Early periods such as the Xia, Shang, and Zhou dynasties lasted hundreds of years and produced a great wealth of art and literature, although the much later Ming dynasty is better known because they made such nice vases.

6

The Egyptians built their great pyramids in about 2500 BC, proving that by this stage of history mankind was able to build a really big pile of rocks. Many people have looked for secret meanings in the pyramids – maps of the stars, messages to aliens, and so on. The boring truth is they are just huge tombs for some egotistical pharaohs who wanted the world to remember their names.

7

South America was home to several spectacular ancient civilizations, including the Mayans, the Aztecs and the Incas. The Spanish killed most of them when they went looking for gold in the fifteenth and sixteenth centuries but some elements of each civilization survived – usually by hiding in the rainforest or the mountains and waiting for the Spaniards to go away.

8

As well as the famous Greek and Roman cultures, early Mediterranean cultures included the Etruscans, Phoenicians, and Hittites. But most people skip these cultures when they read about history because there's only so many ancient civilizations one person can be bothered with. Right?

9

The first kingdom of Israel was at its height around 900 BC. It was conquered by the Assyrians, while the southern kingdom of Judah was conquered by the Babylonians, which may explain why Assyria and Babylon get such a bad press in the Bible.

10

From about 3000 BC onwards, more and more cultures and empires started to spring up around the world, and to start wars with one another. The Indus Valley civilization, the Kush of Africa, the Persians, the Mongols, and the Huns – even Armenia had an empire at one point. By the time of Christ, human civilization was well and truly established around the world, for better or for worse.

Future Bingo

The future history of the world is hard to predict. But as we look forward in fear and hope, why not have some fun while we're waiting?

Keep this **Future Bingo** sheet to hand, and cross off any events that actually happen in the future. If you get a full page of amazing future events, then shout out "House".

If you send the finished page to the **Future Bingo** corporation (at an address yet to be determined), you may even receive a mystery prize . . .

Fort Knox infested by giant gold-eating cockroaches.	Having second head grafted on is the latest fashion.
Husband admits to having to read map upside down.	Wife admits true cost of new pair of shoes.
Aliens bring cure for common cold, destroy Seattle.	Kissing in public outlawed in Sweden.

Chapter Nine

Religious Mania

Saint Lawrence AD ?–258

Saint Lawrence was a church deacon during the reign of
Emperor Valerian (AD 253–60), was responsible for keeping
watch over the church's possessions. He was arrested one day
and ordered by a prefect to hand the church treasures over to the
government. Lawrence agreed but explained that he would need
eight days to assemble them. On the eighth day, Lawrence
visited the prefect and presented him with hundreds of
impoverished and disabled men, women, and children. "These,"
he said, "are the riches of the church." The official was
apparently so enraged that he promptly ordered Lawrence to be
stripped, bound, and slowly roasted to death above a bed of
coals.

St Augustine of Hippo AD 354–430

St Augustine was an Algerian Christian theologian and
philosopher and the Bishop of Hippo, Algeria from AD 396 to
430. Rumour has it that he was once asked, "What was God
doing through all the eternity of time before He created heaven
and earth?" "Creating hell," he is said to have replied, "for those
who ask questions like you."

? ! ? ! ? ! ? ! ? ! ? ! ? ! ? ! ?

FASCINATING FACTS

The Persians and the Greeks
Ancient Greece

Around 490 BC, the Persians (who lived in the area which now comprises Iran) were persistently trying to take the Greeks' land. They built a bridge of boats to cross the Hellespont, a stretch of water between Greece and Asia Minor. They had such a huge army that it took them seven days to walk to Greece across the boats. When the Greeks beat the Persian army at Marathon in 490 BC, the Greeks suffered only 192 dead soldiers but the Persians lost 6,400 men. The tactics of the Greeks were far superior to those of the Persians.

? ! ? ! ? ! ? ! ? ! ? ! ? ! ? ! ?

The Donatists

The Donatists of fourth-century North Africa were so committed to martyrdom that they would stop strangers and demand, on pain of death, to be killed on the spot.

Grisly Tales from History

The Velvet Potty

The Tudors 15th to early 17th Centuries

During King Henry VIII's reign people in general were still indulging into some nasty habits left over from medieval times. People defecated into chamber pots and then threw the contents out of their windows into the streets, regardless of who was walking outside! However, apparently, Henry VIII used a velvet, padded box which had a potty concealed inside. He had a servant with him to clean him and the potty afterwards, called the Yeoman of the Stool.

Babies were often kept in tightly bound bundles for the first few months of their life, to make their bones grow straight. The remedy for teething was to rub a mixture of hare's brains, goose fat, and honey on their gums or a good chew on a horse's tooth. Not surprisingly infant mortality was high. Only one in three babies grew into adulthood.

Give me chastity . . .
In repenting his sinful youth, St Augustine once prayed: "Give me chastity and continence," he pleaded, "but not yet."

Ptolemy I, circa 367–283 BC
Ptolemy I was King of Macedonia, a general under Alexander the Great and the ruler of Egypt between 323 and 285 BC. In 320 BC, an army led by Ptolemy attacked Jerusalem. The city – which had withstood the formidable Sennacherib and Nebuchadnezzar with admirable tenacity – fell easily. Why? The Egyptians had attacked on a holy day and, unlike the Israelis in 1973, the ultra-pious Jews of yore refused to fight on the Sabbath, even in self-defence.

Weird News Stories
DAYLIGHT SWING

Benjamin Franklin suggested that clocks should be moved forward in spring to save daylight hours. He died in 1790, but his idea was not adopted in America and Europe until the First World War, to save electricity.

Hypatia circa AD 370–415

Hypatia, the female Neo-Platonist philosopher, mathematician, and astronomer was the last recorded member of the great museum of Alexandria in Egypt and the only noted scholar of ancient times. Though several Christian bishops were among her pupils, her adherence to pagan scholasticism literally led to her undoing at the hands of Christian zealots. Hypatia was murdered one day by a mob of fanatical monks, who are said to have sliced her body to pieces with oyster shells gathered from the Alexandrian harbour.

Saint Patrick

Saint Patrick, who was born in Ireland (or possibly Wales) around AD 389 and died in AD 461, was a Christian missionary and is the patron saint of Ireland.

During the baptism of King Aengus in the fifth century, St Patrick leaned on his sharp-pointed staff and inadvertently stabbed the king in the foot.

After the ceremony was over, Patrick suddenly realized what he had done when he saw a growing pool of blood and begged the king's forgiveness. "Why did you suffer this pain in silence," he asked. The king allegedly replied: "I thought it was part of the ritual!"

Theodoric the Great circa AD 454–526

Theodoric, who founded the Ostrogoth kingdom in Italy in AD 493, ruled until his death in AD 526. He is noted for his court at Ravenna, the centre of late Roman culture. Theodoric's trusted Catholic minister, hoping to ingratiate himself with the king, one day declared that he was renouncing his Catholicism to embrace the kings Arian faith. Theodoric was not impressed. "If this man is not faithful to his God," he remarked, "how can he be faithful to me, a mere man?" He had the minister beheaded.

Weird News Stories
ON YOUR CHEST

The practice of tapping a patient's chest was invented by an Austrian doctor, Leopold Auenbrugger, who used to watch his father – a wine manufactrer – tapping wine barrels to find out how full they were. Although he published the idea in 1761, it was ignored until his book was translated into French in 1808.

St Beuno ?–circa 440

St Beuno was the Welsh abbot of Clynnog in North Wales in the first half of the fifth century AD. When a chapel in which Saint Beuno's bones were supposedly buried was renovated, it became necessary to open the tomb itself. An anthropologist, invited to inspect the saint's skeleton, was surprised to find that its pelvis apparently contained what appeared to be bones from a fetus. "Well," the supervisor of the renovation is reported to have said, "Saint Beuno was a very remarkable man."

Leo VII AD ?–939

Apparently, Catholic Popes have not always lived up to the rigorous standards they expect from their congregations. Several historians have criticized the Roman Catholic Church for its sale of indulgences (basically a licence to sin). Though the Church espouses celibacy, Popes Leo VII (AD 936–939), Leo VIII (AD 963–964), and Paul II (Pietro Barbo, AD 1467–1471) all died while having sex.

Weird News Stories

HOUSE COUSINS

All thoroughbred race horses in the world are descended from three Eastern horses imported into England in the early eighteenth century: the Byerly Turk, the Darley Arabian, and the Godolphin Barb. Although 174 sires are mentioned in the first General Stud Book, these are the only three whose descent has remained intact.

Canute

Canute, also known as Cnut or Knut, the Great, lived from approximately AD 994 to 1035. He was King of England between AD 1016 and 1035, King of Denmark between AD 1018 and 1035, and King of Norway from AD 1028 to 1035.

According to a twelfth-century chronicle, King Canute, became tired of the excessive flattery of his retainers and ordered that his chair be brought to the seashore, where he commanded the waves not to touch him. Naturally, the incoming tide soon demonstrated the futility of human demands. Canute thereafter hung his crown upon a statue of the crucified Christ to point out that he was not as all powerful as his people had supposed him to be.

Grisly Tales from History

High Church

16th Century

Henry VIII created the Church of England in order to divorce his first wife Catherine of Aragon (she was Catholic and divorce for her was forbidden). He married Anne Boleyn soon after his divorce and she gave birth to a baby girl, Elizabeth, who would grow up to become Queen Elizabeth I. Henry wasn't happy in this marriage either and had Anne Boleyn beheaded. He brought in a special French executioner (who used a sword rather than an axe) to do the deed. His next wife Jane Seymour died in childbirth giving birth to a son, Edward. The next Queen of England was Anne of Cleves whom he married in 1540. He divorced this one after claiming he was disappointed that she was not as pretty in real life as her portrait, which until the marriage was all he had seen of her. He then went on to marry Catherine Howard. Catherine Howard, however, started seeing someone else in secret and, when he found out, Henry had her beheaded, too. Henry VIII's final wife was Catherine Parr who outlived her husband by a year.

St Hugh of Lincoln circa 1135–1200

St Hugh, the Bishop of Lincoln, tried to acquire a sample from a bone said to derive from the arm of Mary Magdalen during a visit to the celebrated monastery of Fecamp. A biographer later recalled that the bone had never been taken from its wrappings by the abbot or the monks present at the time. It was said to have been sewn very tightly into three cloths, two of silk and one of ordinary linen. No monks dared to accede even to the bishop's prayer to be allowed to see it. St Hugh, however, took a small knife from one of his notaries, and hurriedly cut the thread to undo the wrappings. He examined it and apparently then kissed it. He then tried unsuccessfully to break it with his fingers, then with his teeth. By this means he broke off two fragments, which he handed immediately to the writer.

Richard the Lionheart

Richard I, the Lionheart, (AD 1157–1199) was King of England between AD 1189 and 1199, noted for his leadership of the Third Crusade between AD 1190 and 1192 and for his capture and imprisonment in Austria by Holy Roman Emperor Henry VI.

An eminent preacher is said to have once admonished Richard I to marry off his three daughters, lest he be severely punished by God. The king protested that he had no daughters. "Your Majesty has three," the priest apparently replied: "Ambition, avarice, and luxury. Get rid of them as fast as possible, else assuredly some great misfortune will be the consequence."

"If it must be so," Richard retorted, "I give my ambition to the templars, my avarice to the monks, and my luxury to the prelates."

? ! ? ! ? ! ? ! ? ! ? ! ? ! ?

FASCINATING FACTS

No More Words
Ancient Greece

Did you know that the Greeks forgot how to write during the Dark Ages? It was only when they started trading with the Phoenicians (from the area which we now know as Lebanon) around 800 BC that they started to write things down again. However, the Phoenician alphabet contained no vowels so the Greeks added extra signs for the vowels and so started the alphabet, as we know it today. The Greeks gave the Phoenicians their name from the Greek word for purple "Phoinikes" because they made purple dye.

? ! ? ! ? ! ? ! ? ! ? ! ? ! ?

Caesarius of Heisterbach circa 1170–1240

The medieval Cistercian monk and chronicler Caesarius of Heisterbach was apparently amused to overhear a Cistercian lay brother praying: "Lord, if Thou free me not from this temptation, I will complain of Thee to Thy mother."

St Francis of Assisi circa 1182–1226

St Francis of Assisi was an Italian friar, noted for his dissipated youth and for his later conversion in AD 1205 and devotion to prayer and charity. He was declared the patron saint of ecology in 1980.

He is said to have visited Egypt in 1269, intending to convert the sultan, al-Malik al-Kamil, to Christianity. The sultan, however, had laid a trap for him: a carpet, decorated with crosses, placed before his divan. "If he treads on the crosses," the sultan explained, "I will accuse him of insulting his God, and if he refuses to tread on the carpet, I will accuse him of insulting me."

Sure enough, Francis stepped upon the carpet, prompting an outburst from the delighted sultan. Francis, however, was not easily duped: "Our Lord was crucified between two thieves," he apparently declared "We Christians have the True Cross. The crosses of the thieves we have left to you, and I am not ashamed to tread on those."

Simon de Montfort, Earl of Leicester circa AD 1208–1265
Simon de Montfort was a French-born, English nobleman. When the French army, under the guidance of Pope Innocent III, took the town of Beziers near the Mediterranean coast during the Albigensian Crusade in 1209, the question arose as to how its upstanding Christian inhabitants could be distinguished from the damned heretics. It is said that Simon de Montfort had the solution. He ordered them all to be killed pointing out, "The Lord will know his own." As a result, tens of thousands of men, women, and children were indiscriminately slaughtered.

Catherine of Siena 1347–1380
When St Catherine of Siena, an Italian religious leader noted for her mediation of the peace agreement between the Florentines and Pope Urban VI in 1378, was a young novice of the Sisters of Penance, she supposedly nursed a woman with breast cancer. The lesions were suppurating and gave off a nauseating smell. Because she aspired to dominate her physical sensations in the name of submission to God's higher power, the future Doctor of the Church drained some of the fluid into a ladle and drank it. That night, it is rumoured that Jesus came to her in a vision and invited her to drink the blood spurting from His wounds.

127

Weird News Stories

FOREIGN LANGUAGE

It is 1870. She is Gretchen Gottlieb, a sixteen-year-old Catholic girl, terrified and in hiding from anti-Catholic fanatics in a forest. "The man made my mother dead," she says. She complains that her head aches, she talks about a glittering knife, and then, desperately, evades questions. "Gretchen can't," she finally wails. And there it ends. Gretchen presumably was killed, and Mrs Jay remembers nothing until her own life began in 1923. Mrs Dolores Jay is an ordinary American housewife, married to a minister and the mother of four children. But when she is deeply hypnotized, Dolores Jay moves back through time past the time of her childhood and her infancy – deeper and deeper back until she whimpers in German. (When she is conscious, she neither speaks nor understands any German.) Dolores Jay herself can't account for it. She doesn't believe in reincarnation. She has only heard fragments of the taped hypnosis sessions, but she can't understand the language. She has never been to Germany. She has never heard of the little town of Eberswalde where Gretchen says she lived, and which exists in what is now East Germany close to the Polish border. But Eberswalde was the scene of Germany's last stand against the Soviet Union in 1945, and the town was almost completely razed. The records that once might have proved whether or not there was such a person as Gretchen Gottlieb have been destroyed.

128

GRAMMATICAL ERROR

The misplacing of a comma cost the United States treasury over a million dollars. In the Tariff Act of 1872, "fruit plants, tropical and semi-tropical" were exempted from tax. A clerk miscopied it: "fruit, plants tropical and semi-tropical." Importers contended that this meant that tropical and semitropical fruits should be exempted. The treasury disagreed and collected the tax, but finally gave way and refunded over a million dollars. The wording was then changed.

Calixtus III AD 1378–1458

Halley's comet could be seen in the night sky on 29 June 1456 and people feared it presaged a plague, famine, or some other disaster. The Italian Pope Calixtus III, who had ruled for one year, issued a papal bull or official decree against the comet. His decree asked Christendom to pray that the comet – or symbol of "the anger of God," as he allegedly put it – be diverted from Earth or that, as Bartolomeo Platina wrote in 1479, the comet "be entirely diverted against the Turks, the foes of the Christian name."

Bracciolini Gian Francesco Poggio 1380–1459

Italian humanist scholar and writer Bracciolini Poggio – as a secretary in the papal Curia – wore ecclesiastical dress though he was never ordained a priest. It is said that a cardinal once chided him for having children, pointing out that this was unbecoming of a man in clerical garb. He was also disapproved of for having a mistress, which the cardinal noted was unbecoming even of a layman.

"I have children, which is suitable for a layman," Poggio supposedly retorted. "And I have a mistress, which is a time-honoured custom of the clergy."

Grisly Tales from History

The Disposable Castle

16th Century

After becoming Queen in 1558, Elizabeth I moved her court and courtiers around the country a lot, staying in large noble houses and castles. This is now thought to be due to a lack of personal hygiene, fleas, and disease. The place would eventually become very smelly and need a good clean which was why the Royal party moved on . . . the cleaners then moved in to get rid of all the accumulated dirt and rubbish.

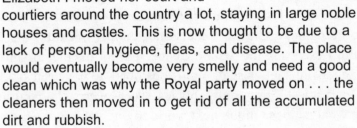

Julius II AD 1443–1513

In 1505, Italian pope Julius II, born Giuliano della Rovere
Savona, quarreled with Michelangelo, who was forced into a
year-long project to create a giant bronze statue of the man.
When the sculptor suggested depicting the Pope with his right
hand raised and a book in his left, Julius demurred. "Put a sword
there," he demanded, "for I know nothing of letters." The statue
was later melted down – fittingly so that the bronze could be
used to build cannons.

Weird News Stories

GIANT SHOW

In Montana, snowflakes fifteen
inches across and eight inches
thick fell during a record
snowstorm in the winter of 1887.

Pietro di Cristoforo Vannucci Perugino 1446–1523

Pietro Perugino, an Italian Renaissance painter noted for his
graceful frescoes in the Sistine Chapel and for his mentorship of
the painter Raphael, is said, on his deathbed, to have refused to
send for a priest. Supposedly, his last words were, "I am curious
to see what happens in the next world to one who dies
unshriven."

? ! ? ! ? ! ? ! ? ! ? ! ? ! ? ! ?

FASCINATING FACTS

Sparta
Ancient Greece

Sparta was a state in the south of Greece known for producing very tough people. In school boys who didn't do well enough or pay enough attention to the teacher were badly beaten. Girls were not allowed to go to school but were encouraged to run and be athletic and active. It is rumoured that Spartan girls wore their skirts much shorter than the rest of Greece to help with all the running!

? ! ? ! ? ! ? ! ? ! ? ! ? ! ? ! ?

Leonardo da Vinci 1452–1519
While working on "The Last Supper," Leonardo da Vinci is said to have remarked that if he could not find a face to paint that was sufficiently evil for Judas he would happily substitute that of the prior in whose abbey he was working.

Desiderius Erasmus circa 1466–1536
It is said that Erasmus, the Dutch Renaissance humanist scholar and Roman Catholic theologian, was once reproached for having failed to observe the Lenten fast. His supposed response was, "I have a Catholic soul, but a Lutheran stomach!"

Weird News Stories
SENIOR FISTICUFFS

In 1822, Thomas Dawson, ninety-one, and Michael O'Toole, eighty-five, engaged in fisticuffs to settle an argument and "fought to a finish" in Garford, Berks. O'Toole collapsed first, but ninety-one-year-old Dawson died a few hours later.

Michelangelo Buonarroti 1475–1564
Michelangelo, the Italian Renaissance sculptor, painter, architect, and poet, was frequently pestered by Pope Paul III's master of ceremonies while painting his famous "Last Judgment" fresco in the Vatican's Sistine Chapel. The man is said to have wanted a glimpse of the emerging masterpiece. When the work was unveiled at last, the man found himself depicted in the painting among the damned in hell, being tormented by demons. The man was horrified and promptly complained to the Pope, who supposedly refused to intervene. He is said to have declared "God has given me authority in Heaven and on Earth, but my writ does not extend to Hell."

Hugh Latimer circa 1485–1555
Hugh Latimer was an English bishop and Protestant martyr noted for his part in the Oxford disputations against a group of Catholic theologians in 1554 and for his refusal to recant his

Protestant faith. When he and Nicholas Ridley, the Bishop of London, were condemned to be burned at the stake after their show trial for heresy in 1555, as the fire was lit, Latimer turned to the bishop and said, "Be of good comfort, Master Ridley, and play the man," he advised. "We shall this day light such a candle, by God's grace, in England as I trust shall never be put out."

Grisly Tales from History

Blood and Bondages
16th Century

Barbers traditionally had red and white striped poles outside their shops. This was supposed to represent blood and bandages. The custom dated from the fifteenth and sixteenth centuries. Barbers used razors, but not only to cut hair. They were also used to cut off other things such as gangrenous toes or other appendages and also to lance boils to let the pus out.

Pope Julius III 1487–1555

Born Giammaria Ciocchi del Monte, Italian pope Julius III supposedly asked a shoemaker to fashion special papal slippers. When they were presented to the new Pope for a fitting, they were found to be too small. The shoemaker apologized, "I am afraid they don't fit you, Holy Father." Apparently the Pope replied, "On the contrary, no shoes ever fitted me better than these in my life."

Weird News Stories

DOPED AMERICANS

There were more opium addicts in America – per head of population – in 1865 than there are today. During the Civil War, opium was used as an anaesthetic during operations, and created 100,000 addicts in a population of 40 million. Today, with a population of 200 million, there are about 300,000 addicts.

Michael Servetus 1511–1553

The Spanish-born theologian and physician Michael Servetus (born Miguel Serveto) was declared a heretic for his denial of the doctrine of the Trinity and narrowly escaped the Inquisition in Calvin's Geneva. However, he was eventually caught, tried for heresy, and condemned to be burned to death at the stake. "I will burn, but this is a mere incident," he declared before his judges. "We shall continue our discussion in eternity."

St Teresa of Avila 1515–1582
St Teresa was a Spanish Carmelite nun and writer noted for her
foundation of convents at Avila, in 1562, and, with the aid of
St John of the Cross, several other religious communities in
which the reformed Carmelite rule was practised. On one
occasion St Teresa was approached by a young nun who
confessed to a plenitude of spiritual tribulations and terrible
sins. After listening to her for some time, Saint Teresa gave her
a word of advice: "We know, sister, that none of us is perfect,"
she said. "Just take care that your sins don't turn into bad
habits."

Mary, Queen of Scots 1542–1587
Mary was the daughter of James V of Scotland. she is noted
for her forced abdication in favour of her one-year-old son,
James VI, later James I of England, and her imprisonment
and execution, ordered by Elizabeth I, for her complicity
in the Babington plot of 1586. Mary was famously devoutly
religious. It is said that the linen sheets upon which
she slept were fashioned from the fibers of stinging nettle
plants.

Greedy Pig
17th–18th Century

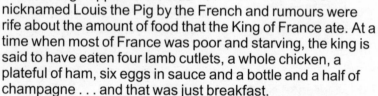

Louis XVI of France fell out of
favour with his courtiers and public
over his huge appetite. He was
nicknamed Louis the Pig by the French and rumours were
rife about the amount of food that the King of France ate. At a
time when most of France was poor and starving, the king is
said to have eaten four lamb cutlets, a whole chicken, a
plateful of ham, six eggs in sauce and a bottle and a half of
champagne . . . and that was just breakfast.

Things got so bad that in July 1789, an angry mob
attacked the infamous Bastille jail in Paris and let out all
the prisoners. The leaders of what is now known as the
French Revolution quickly arrested all members of the
royal court and sentenced them to death. They executed
them using a guillotine, a tall weighted axe that dropped
onto the neck of the accused, chopping off their head. The
head then fell into a basket. The executioner would hold up
the head and the gathered crowd of spectators would
cheer. After the King and his wife Marie-Antoinette were
executed, beheadings became a major French pastime.
Anyone who looked like they might be getting a bit too
much power was likewise sent to the guillotine. As angry
mobs rioted through the streets, heads were cut off and
carried aloft on pikes. The instigators of the revolution
were almost all eventually accused and beheaded
themselves.

In the French town off Nantes, the citizens all refused
to accept the new Revolutionary government and were
all sentenced to death. To guillotine them all would
take too long so they were taken on a barge into the
middle of the river and the barge was sunk, drowning
them all.

137

Weird News Stories

DR FRANKENSTEIN

Mary Shelley's novel *Frankenstein*, written in 1816, was based on a real scientist, Andrew Crosse, whose lectures on electricity were attended by the poet Shelley and his wife in 1814. But twenty-one years after the novel was written, Crosse suddenly achieved notoriety when he announced that he had actually created life in his laboratory. In 1837, he decided to try and make crystals of natural glass; he made glass out of ground flint and potassium carbonate, and dissolved it in sulphuric acid. He then allowed the mixture to drip through a piece of porous iron oxide from mount Vesuvius which was "electrified" by a battery. After two weeks, tiny white nipples began to grow out of the stone, and these turned into hairy legs. When he noticed that they were moving he examined them through a microscope and saw what appeared to be tiny bugs. He thought there might be tiny insect eggs in the porous stone, so he sealed his carefully sterilized mixture into an airtight retort and passed electricity through it. In a few months, he again had tiny "bugs". A paper on his "discovery", read to the London Electrical Society, caused him to be violently denounced by clergymen as a blasphemer. Meanwhile the great Michael Faraday repeated Crosse's experiments and obtained the same "bugs". Crosse withdrew and led a hermit-like existence until his death in 1855. The mystery of the "bugs" has never been solved.

Galileo Galilei 1564–1642

Galileo was an Italian astronomer and physicist noted for his pioneering use of the telescope to study the stars, in 1610, his espousal of Copernicus's geocentric theory of the solar system, and for his consequent persecution and imprisonment by the Inquisition in 1633. Even though the theory had been pronounced a heresy, Galileo published his *Dialogue on Two Chief World Systems* in 1632. He had made a number of important astronomical discoveries that convinced him of the validity of Nicholas Copernicus's geocentric theory (that the earth moves around the sun rather than the reverse). The Inquisition promptly summoned him to Rome, where he reluctantly recanted and was sentenced to house arrest for the rest of his life. As he rose from his knees after his solemn renunciation of the Copernican doctrine, however, he is said to have muttered: "Eppur si muove!" (But still it moves!)

Johann Bayer 1572–1625

Because he felt it was blasphemous to name constellations after characters from Greek mythology, the sixteenth-century German astronomer Johann Bayer introduced a new system in which the northern constellations were named after New Testament characters and the southern constellations after Old Testament characters. Needless to say, the scheme did not catch on.

James I 1566–1625

James I was King of England and Ireland between 1603 and 1625, and of Scotland, as James VI, between 1567 and 1625. He was the son of Mary, Queen of Scots. According to history, a preacher famed for his fearless social criticism was invited to speak before King James I in the sixteenth century. The man stood in the pulpit and began: "James One, Six. 'But let him ask

in faith, nothing wavering. For he that wavereth is like a wave of the sea, driven with the wind and tossed.'"
"God's faith!" the king is said to have cried. "He's at me already."

? ! ? ! ? ! ? ! ? ! ? ! ? ! ?

FASCINATING FACTS

Party On

Ancient Greece

Festivals and drinking parties were very popular with the Ancient Greeks. They played a game called cottabos. This seems to have involved throwing what was left in your wine cup at a chosen target. The person with the most direct hit was the winner. Knucklebones was a game played mostly by girls. The bones were the ankle bones of goats which were thrown into the air and then caught on the back of the hand. They even had a version of snakes and ladders!

? ! ? ! ? ! ? ! ? ! ? ! ? ! ?

James Ussher 1581–1655

While working on his chronology of the Bible, *Annales Veteris et Novi Testamenti* one day in the mid-seventeenth century, Irish bishop James Ussher is said to have calculated what he believed to be the precise time of the Creation. His estimate was very precise indeed: Sunday 23 October 4004 BC – at 9.00 am!

Weird News Stories

GIANT BUDDHA

The largest statue of the Buddha in the world is in Pegu, Burma – it is 180 feet long and is in a reclining position. The statue was lost for 400 years: all records of it vanish around the middle of the fifteenth century, and it was not found again until 1881, when a railway was being built. The statue was covered with earth and vegetation.

Dr Daniel Price, Dean of Hereford 17th Century

Regular processions were organized around Hereford Cathedral to mark holy occasions at the end of the sixteenth century. Prior to one such procession the Dean of Hereford, Dr Price, decided that in view of his own importance he would not, as had previously been common, walk on foot with the rest of the lowlier canons. He decided instead to ride on horseback so that he might more easily be seen reading from his prayer book. The proud cleric mounted his mare, opened his book and took to the streets. His reading was at an early stage when a stallion broke loose, saw his mare and mounted her. The dean was trapped, read practically nothing and swore he would never ride in a procession again.

Raimund Montecuccoli, Duke of Melfi 1609–1680
The Austrian general Raimund Montecuccoli, an observant Roman Catholic, ordered an omelet for dinner one Friday evening, when, as a Catholic, he should have been eating fish rather than meat. He was unusually hungry and saw no harm in adding a few small slices of ham to the meal. As his meal was served, a very loud clap of thunder issued from the darkened sky, clearly the start of a violent storm. Silently, the general stood up, marched across the room, and threw his omelet through the nearest window. "What a lot of noise for a ham omelet!" he is said to have exclaimed, gazing heavenward.

Grisly Tales from History

Russia Under Siege

17th Century

In 1664, Tzar Dmitri was allegedly told that a comet seen over Russia was an indication of a plague which would reach Russia that autumn, though it would harm Russia less than other countries. Dmitri promptly set up a sanitary cordon round Russia's borders and banned foreign ships in general (and English ships in particular) from entering Russian ports. Interestingly, Russia did in fact escape the Great Plague that devastated the rest of Europe in 1666.

Jean-Baptiste Poquelin Molière 1622–1673

On 17 February 1673, French playwright and actor Molière, although desperately ill, insisted on perfoming in a scheduled play rather than let his company down. After the performance he was carried home, where he died a short time later. Given that religious prejudice against the theatre was so strong, it was customary for a dying actor to formally renounce his profession in order to obtain permission for burial in consecrated ground. Molière's sudden death, however, prevented this. Appeals to the archbishop of Paris were rejected, and Molière's grieving widow sought the help of the king. King Louis asked the ecclesiastical authorities how deep into the ground the earth was considered consecrated. The supposed response was fourteen feet. Louis declared that Molière's grave be dug in the churchyard sixteen feet deep where it could be said that he is buried in consecrated ground without scandalizing the clergy. His grave however, has never been found.

Weird News Stories

A MAGIC DIVORCE

Eliphas Lévi, the nineteenth-century writer on theories of magic, seldom practiced what he wrote about. But when he was offered a complete magical chamber, he decided to try to evoke Apollonius of Tyana. Lévi made his circle, kindled the ritual fires, and began reading the evocations of the ritual.

A ghostly figure appeared before the altar. Lévi found himself seized with a great chill. He placed his hand on the pentagram, the five-pointed symbol used to protect magicians against harm. He also pointed his sword at the figure, commanding it mentally to obey and not to alarm him. Something touched the hand holding the sword, and his arm became numb from the elbow down. Lévi realized that the figure objected to the sword, and he lowered it to the ground. At this, a great weakness came over him, and he fainted without having asked his questions.

After his swoon, however, he seemed to have the answers to his unasked questions. He had meant to ask one about the possibility of forgiveness and reconciliation between "two persons who occupied my thought." The answer was, "Dead."

It was his marriage that was dead. His wife, who had recently left him, never returned.

144

WEIRD TALES

Missing in Kansas

A story has it that in the spring of 1872 the Bender family (man, wife and two children, one boy and girl) appeared in Kansas. They constructed a home that was also a general store and a wayside inn to provide both food and a room for travellers. A canvas curtain separated the grocery store and inn from the family's living quarters. Mr Bender and his wife were thought to have been immigrants from Germany but they spoke with such a strange accent that no one could be certain.

Their daughter Kate was outgoing and, it is said, aggressive. She was tall with blonde hair and many men were attracted to her. She became quite a business magnet for the Bender's establishment. She became known in the Kansas region as "Professor Miss Kate Bender", a psychic medium, able to contact the spirits of the dead and even cure illness for a generous donation. Kate appeared in a number of small Kansas towns with her spiritualistic show, giving public séances. Rumour has it that men who traced her back to the Bender establishment were never seen again

Some travelers told of hearing odd noises from behind the curtain as they ate. It is said that if a diner, overnight guest, or séance participant appeared to be wealthy, he was given a seat of honour with his back to the curtain. While Kate distracted him, Mr Bender or his son would sneak up to the curtain with a sledgehammer. They would then strike a savage blow to the top of the man's head, killing him instantly. The body was then dragged back beneath the canvas and stripped. A trap door that led to an earthen cellar was opened and the body was dumped below until it could be buried somewhere on the prairie. This system of murder worked well for around 18 months. Kate drew

145

a number of victims to their door with her offers of spirit communication and her brother often brought back travelers from nearby roads, convincing them to spend the night at their inn.

A short time after his brother's disappearance, on 4 May 1873, Colonel York arrived at the Bender home. He asked the family about whether or not his brother had passed through the area. They said no. Later on that night, while sitting alone in the front room, he happened to notice something glittering underneath one of the beds. It was a locket on a gold chain. He opened it and saw the faces of his brother's wife and daughter inside. York slipped out of the front door intending to notify the authorities. He spotted a lantern swinging back and forth in the dark. York walked in the direction of the light and as he got closer, he saw Mr Bender and his son digging a hole in the ground. Nearby was a large object wrapped in canvas that looked suspiciously like a body.

When York returned with the sheriff and a contingent of deputies and local men from town. When they arrived however, they found that the house was empty. The Benders had packed up and left the place. York inspected the cellar and noted with alarm that the dirt floor was coated with dried blood. The stench of the place was overpowering.

Outside the house they found 11 mounds of oddly shaped earth. The men began to dig and the body of Colonel York's brother was found in the first grave that was opened. More than two dozen bodies were allegedly found. The news soon spread and curiosity-seekers flocked to the house. The tale here varies in its conclusion

Some claim that a small band of riders caught up with the Bender family and killed them. The Benders were all shot except for Kate who was burned alive for her crimes. Others argue that the Benders had managed to escape out on the trackless prairie. By 1886, the house in which the Bender's had lived was reduced to nothing more than an empty hole that had once been the cellar. Relic seekers carried away every last remnant of the building, even taking the stones that lined the cellar walls. Some stories claim that the ghosts of the Bender's victims haunted the ruins of the house and later, the earthen hole that remained. People who wandered out to the site of the house claimed they were often frightened off by strange, glowing apparitions and moaning sounds that came from the darkness. Some of these spirits still allegedly wander the area today.

Weird News Stories

CONGRESSIONAL IDIOCY IN HISTORY

Abraham Lincoln remarked of a congressman: "He can compress the most words into the fewest ideas of anyone I've ever known."

Chapter Ten

A Brief, Unreliable History of . . .
The Greeks

The Greeks

Everything you ever wanted to know about
the civilisation that brought us
philosophy and scandals.

1

Ancient Greece was home to a complex civilization from at least
3000 BC onwards. The first phase of civilization resulted in
Homer's epics recording the tales of Agamemnon and the wars
with Troy. Today Homer is best known for being a character in
The Simpsons.

2

When the Mycaenean Greek civilization fell into the Greek dark
ages from 1100 BC to 800 BC, the Mycaenean written language
was lost and the Greeks needed to borrow an alphabet from the
Phoenicians when they started wanting to write stuff down
again.

3

Early Greek history records the noble and heroic exploits of the
plucky city of Athens in its wars with other cities and islands.
But as the surviving histories were all written by Athenians, it's
best to take them with a big pinch of salt.

4

After the Persian Wars, Athens became the dominant city in the region. As a result it became wealthy and its citizens had more time to devote to art, philosophy and dinner parties than the average man in the street.

5

After a few centuries of Pre-Socratic philosophy, Socrates became famous for explaining in great detail to people why they were wrong and also for suggesting a new Republic to be ruled by a philosopher-king. Perhaps it was the fact that he kept coughing and pointing to himself that irritated people, but either way it's not so surprising that his fellow citizens found him a bit of a nuisance and tried to exile him. He refused the easy option, preferring the drama of a cup of hemlock, and the rest is history.

6

The greatest dramatist of Ancient Athens was Aristophanes. His greatest play was called *The Frogs*. Enough said?

7

The first marathon runner was Pheidippides. He was sent from Marathon to Athens to carry the news that the Battle of Marathon against the Persians had been miraculously won. He ran the whole way there, made his announcement, then keeled over dead of a heart attack. To this day, runners around the world foolishly ignore the obvious moral of this story ("Don't

run that far, dummy, stop for a rest") and emulate Pheidippides'
extraordinary feat.

8

The Olympic Games originated in Ancient Greece and ran for
approximately 400 years from the eighth to the fourth century
BC. Legend has it that Heracles, son of Zeus, built the first
stadium after completing his twelve labours.

9

In 431 BC war broke out between Athens and Sparta. The war
that became known as the Pelopponesian War was fought
between Athens, a city where the citizens liked to lie around
eating grapes and discussing philosophy, and Sparta, a city
where citizens were trained in the brutal art of hand-to-hand
warfare from infancy. Three guesses who won?

10

Sparta's dominance was surprisingly short-lived. Possibly
because the Spartans liked fighting too much and were no good
at the subsequent hassle of ruling the cities they had conquered.
As a result Spartan hegemony fizzled out and Athens and
Thebes came back into the ring. But by this stage the Greek
civilization was in decline anyway, and before too long the
Romans would rise to far greater power than the Greeks had
ever achieved.

153

Future Bingo

The future history of the world is hard to predict. But as we look forward in fear and hope, why not have some fun while we're waiting?

Keep this **Future Bingo** sheet to hand, and cross off any events that actually happen in the future. If you get a full page of amazing future events, then shout out "House".

If you send the finished page to the **Future Bingo** corporation (at an address yet to be determined), you may even receive a mystery prize . . .

Walt Disney reanimated.	Zombies attack Midwest shopping mall.
Miniature dinosaur found hiding in Mexican well.	Bat-cow hybrid cloned by bored teenage genius.
Squirrel finds buried nuts.	Mud Wrestling World Championships cancelled due to lack of interest.

Chapter Ten

Weird News: Pirate Ladies

On 28 November 1720 a court in London was called to pass sentence on a large number of pirates who had all been captured in Jamaica. A certain Lieutenant Barret testified that he had caught the whole band of brigands by boarding their boat off the north coast of the island and they had all been so unprofessionally drunk that they had all, except two, offered no resistance.

The whole crew were thus hauled to London in chains, the two who had put up a fight being most securely manacled. One of the two had even fired a shot at members of his own crew, enraged at their lack of masculinity in the face of adversity. All the other sailors had conceded defeat meekly, most being incapable of coherent speech

The death sentence was declared on every single member of the crew and the court went through the ritual of asking if anyone knew of a good reason why this should not be carried out. Normally this question was met with stony silence. On this occasion, however, the two boisterous young lads who had been the only ones to offer resistance called out the age-old expression "Milord, we plead our bellies." This was greeted with hoots of derisory laughter since it was the phrase used by young ladies to indicate that they were pregnant and thus could not be hanged. Everyone in the tribunal naturally considered that this was part of the general ribald exchange for which pirates were notorious and carried on laughing but the sailors would not give up. Eventually a court physician was called in to examine the two young men. He came back to the court to announce to a stunned audience and even more stunned crew that the two young men were, in fact, two young women and both were pregnant. The two women, whose stories are now well-known, were called Ann Bonny and Mary Read and both had succeeded in being mistaken for men over an admirably long period of time.

SKID ROW

The term "skid row" was first used in the lumberjacking days in Seattle. The logs were sent from a hilltop down a long chute and into the sea. Around the lower end of this chute there was a slum area where drunks and down-and-outs often slept in the gutter. This area became known as "skid row" after the logs that skidded down the chute.

WEIRD TALES

The Devil's Footprints

The winter of 1855 was an exceptionally severe one, even in the southwest of England, where winters are usually mild. On the morning of 8 February Albert Brailsford, the principal of the village school in Topsham, Devon, walked out of his front door to find that it had snowed in the night. And he was intrigued to notice a line of footprints – or rather hoof prints – that ran down the village street. At first glance they looked like the ordinary hoof prints of a shod horse; but a closer look showed that this was impossible, for the prints ran in a continuous line, one in front of the other. If it was a horse, then it must have had only one leg, and hopped along the street. And if the unknown creature had two legs, then it must have placed one carefully in front of the other, as if walking along a tightrope.

What was odder still was that the prints – each about four inches long – were only about eight inches apart. And each print was very clear, as if it had been branded into the frozen snow with a hot iron. The villagers of Topsham were soon following the track southward through the snow. They halted in astonishment when the hoof prints came to a halt at a brick wall. Then, someone discovered that they continued on the other side of the wall, and that the snow on top of the wall was undisturbed. The tracks approached a haystack, and continued on the other side of it, although the hay showed no sign that a heavy creature had clambered over it. The prints passed under gooseberry bushes, and were even seen on rooftops. It began to look as if some insane practical joker had decided to set the village an insoluble puzzle. But it was soon clear that this explanation was also out of the question.

Excited investigators tracked the prints for mile after mile over the Devon countryside. They seemed to wander erratically

160

through a number of small towns and villages – Lympstone, Exmouth, Teignmouth, Dawlish, as far as Totnes, about halfway to Plymouth. If it was a practical joker, he would have had to cover forty miles, much of it through deep snow. Moreover, such a joker would surely have hurried forward to cover the greatest distance possible; in fact, the steps often approached front doors, then changed their mind and went away again. At some point the creature had crossed the estuary of the river Exe – it looked as if the crossing was between Lympstone and Powderham.

Yet there were also footprints in Exmouth, farther south, as if it had turned back on its tracks. There was no logic in its meandering course. In places it looked as if the "horseshoe" had a split in it, suggesting a cloven hoof. It was the middle of the Victorian era, and few country people doubted the existence of the Devil. Men armed with guns and pitchforks followed the trail; when night came people locked their doors and kept loaded shotguns at hand.

A week later the press picked up the story. Many people tried to offer information as to what the creature could be, explanations were given from a badger to a kangaroo and even a rat!

The likeliest hypothesis is one put forward by Geoffrey Household, who edited a small book containing all the major correspondence on the matter. He comments as follows, in a letter to the local paper:

I think that Devonport dockyard released, by accident, some sort of experimental balloon. It broke free from its moorings, and trailed two shackles on the end of ropes. The impression left in the snow by these shackles went up the sides of houses, over haystacks, etc. . . . . A Major Carter, a local man, tells me that his grandfather worked at Devonport at the time, and that the whole thing was hushed up because the balloon destroyed a number of conservatories, greenhouses, windows, etc. He says that the balloon finally came down at Honiton.

The fact that it took a week for the first report of the mystery to appear in print means that certain vital clues have been lost for ever. It would be interesting to know, for example, whether the snow that fell that night was the first snow of February 1855. It had been a hard winter that year, and many small animals, including rats, rabbits, and badgers, must have been half starved by February, and have been out looking for food. The letter to the Plymouth Gazette (dated 17 February) begins: "Thursday night, the 8th of February, was marked by a heavy fall of snow, followed by rain and boisterous wind from the east, and in the morning frost." Small animals had probably been out every night, but it was not until that Friday morning, with its fresh carpet of snow, that their tracks were noticed for the first time. Such tracks would have sunk deep into the soft snow, and would have been further deepened by the rain before they were frozen solid. This would explain why they seemed to be "branded" into the snow.

But if the ground was already covered with snow before the night of 8 February, then one more plausible theory would have to be abandoned. And in any case it fails to explain how the tracks managed to wander over rooftops and haystacks . . . At this distance in time, the only certainty seems to be that the mystery is now insoluble.

GATS

The word "gat" – American slang for a gun – was derived from the Gatling gun, the world's first machine-gun, which was invented during the American Civil War by Richard Jordan Gatling.

Chapter Twelve

A Brief, Unreliable History of . . .
The Romans

The Romans

Everything you ever wanted to know about
the empire that brought us Caligula
and his horse.

1

Legend has it that Roman civilization was founded by two
brothers. Romulus and Remus were descendants of a Trojan
Prince and the god Mars, who had his wicked way with their
mother. Since this made them half-god, the new king had them
drowned, but they survived and were brought up by wolves on
the Italian peninsula.

2

The early Romans were ruled by the Etruscans, but after the
Etruscan civilization waned, the Sabine and Latin tribes formed
their own republic, a form of government in which all the
citizens are involved. Except the plebeians and the slaves, of
course.

3

The Romans quickly became successful at quelling their
neighbours and taxing them, and thus the city grew into a
powerful presence in the region. When the Romans came to

visit, the only two things that were certain was that they would bring death and taxes.

4

After the Social War, Sulla became the dictator of Rome. This led to the collapse of the original Roman Republic in a Civil War. Originally there had been further wars planned with titles such as the Friendly War and the Charming War, but these plans were cancelled once Julius Caesar came on to the scene.

5

Caesar first rose to power as part of a triumvirate with Pompey and Crassus, but shared power didn't suit Caesar so he took the unprecedented step of declaring himself Dictator for Life. However, this life was eventually cut short at the hands of Brutus.

6

Caesar's heir Octavian then came to power, marking the start of the Roman Empire. He was given the title of Augustus. We still remember the Caesar family in a variety of ways. We named the months of July and August after the first two Caesars, and the words czar, kaiser and dictator all have their roots in Caesar's seizure of absolute power.

7

The Julio-Claudian dynasty lasted for about 100 years, as a succession of increasingly ridiculous descendants ascended to the post of Emperor.

8

Tiberius was paranoid, Claudius started well, but allowed himself to be made into a god, while Nero was something of a drama queen, best remembered for fiddling while Rome burned. What he was fiddling with is not recorded.

9

However the most spectacular emperor of the period was Caligula, who was splendidly mad. He tried to have his horse appointed to the Senate, ordered his troops to Britain to fight the sea-god, only to change his mind and ask them to collect sea-shells from the beach in Northern France instead, and had anyone to whom he took exception killed. It was no great surprise when his own life ended in assassination.

10

The second century AD marked the high point of the Roman Empire, as the Pax Romana covered most of the continent of Europe, and Rome flourished, in spite of occasional rebellions. But once the wise Marcus Aurelius's nutty son Commodus became emperor the decline of the Empire was underway.

Commodus was eventually killed (by Russell Crowe) but already the barbarians were on the march, and by the third century, Rome's heyday was over.

Future Bingo

The future history of the world is hard to predict. But as we look forward in fear and hope, why not have some fun while we're waiting?

Keep this **Future Bingo** sheet to hand, and cross off any events that actually happen in the future. If you get a full page of amazing future events, then shout out "House".

If you send the finished page to the **Future Bingo** corporation (at an address yet to be determined), you may even receive a mystery prize . . .

Supreme Court rules that gay chickens can marry.	Zombie Woodrow Wilson becomes World President.
Last gallon of world's oil reserves wasted on pointless trip to the mall.	Footbridge across the Pacific opened.
Mice and rats declare truce, start war with cats.	Elvis found alive and well in Dusseldorf.

Chapter Thirteen

Dumbology: Gaffes, Foul-Ups, Blunders, and Oddballs

Buonamico Buffalmacco, Italian painter circa 1262–1340
The painter Buonamico Buffalmacco is said to have once lived
next door to a rich wool worker whose wife worked late at her
spinning wheel, often keeping him awake all night.

   In desperation he devised a plan to solve the problem.
Having noticed a small hole in their kitchen wall directly above
the cooking pot, Buffalmacco hollowed out a cane, pushed it
through the hole, and was thereby able to add a large amount of
salt to the wool worker's dinner.

   When, after two or three such tainted meals, the exasperated
man began to beat his wife for her carelessness, her screams
brought a number of neighbors, including Buffalmacco, to their
door. "This calls for a little reason," the wily painter declared.
"You complain that the pot is too much salted, but I marvel that
this good woman can do anything well, considering that the
whole night she sits up over that wheel of hers and has not an
hour's sleep. Let her give up this all-night work and sleep her
fill, so she will have her wits about her by day and will not fall
into such blunders."

   The woolworker apparently graciously accepted
Buffalmacco's advice, and he was thereafter enjoyed peaceful
rest.

Alfonso X, the Wise circa 1221–1284
Alfonso the Wise, King of Castile and Leon between 1252 and
1284, was famed for his patronage of the arts and sciences, for
his revision of the Castilian legal code, for his sponsorship of
the translation of many Arabic works, and for his compilation of
the "Alfonsine Tables" which remained the most authoritative
planetary tables in existence for some three hundred years.
Because they were based upon a then prevalent but erroneous
Ptolemaic (geocentric) scheme, however, many complicated

calculations were required to render the tables usable. Indeed, Alfonso is said to have remarked that, had God consulted him during the six days of creation, he might have recommended a less complicated design.

Roger Bacon, "Doctor Mirabilis" circa 1214–1292

The thirteenth-century English friar, scientist, and philosopher Roger Bacon once contended that elderly men could be rejuvenated in a curious fashion, by inhaling the breath of young virgins. It is worth noting that, at a time when men were lucky to see their 50th birthdays, Bacon lived to be nearly eighty years old.

Grisly Tales from History

Betting on the Gallows

17th Century

In the seventeenth century, Oliver Cromwell, Lord Protector of England, passed an edict to curtail the savage practices of some of his troops (ranging from rape to pillage and murder). The offending soldier and his entire company would assemble underneath the local gallows and hold a meeting.

At the meeting all the men would participate in rolling the dice. The man who lost would be hanged, whether he had committed the crime or not. The result was fewer crimes, fewer troops – and fewer meetings.

Nizam-ud-din Auliya, Indian saint

In the fourteenth century, Ghiyas-uddin Tughlaq began to build
the third city of Delhi: Tughlaqabad. When Tughlaq
expropriated several workers who had been employed to build a
shrine for the Sufi saint Nizam-ud-din, the saint placed a curse
on the project, prophesying that the city would be inhabited only
by shepherds. The king promptly vowed revenge and began to
march toward Nizam-ud-din's own distant city; the saint calmly
told his followers not to worry. "Delhi," he declared, "is a long
way off" (*Dilli Doorasth*).

His words turned out to be prophetic; the king was murdered
en route from Delhi in 1325. Moreover, the city today is indeed
largely inhabited by shepherds.

Weird News Stories

WASTED INGENUITY

 The invention of transparent
sticky tape was delayed for a
long time because of
unsuccessful attempts to find a
way of preventing the rubber-
based gum from sticking to the
back of the tape when it was
wound into a roll. Finally, it was
discovered that the experiments had been unnecessary:
the gum has a natural tendency to remain only on one side
of the tape.

Pedro I, King of Portugal 14th Century
When Pedro I became King of Portugal in the fourteenth
century, he had his dead mistress exhumed for the coronation.
Having been crowned queen alongside her widowed husband,
she had her hand kissed by many of the noblemen in attendance
before being replaced in her casket and returned to her tomb.

Edward III, 1312–77, King of England 1327–77
At the height of the battle of Crecy, Edward III was told by a
messenger that Edward the Black Prince, his sixteen-year-old
eldest son, was at the forefront of the fighting and in
considerable danger. Edward refused to send reinforcements or
to call his son back from the field of battle. His orders were to,
"Let the boy win his spurs."

Facino Cane, Italian *condottiere* 1360–1412
The fourteenth-century Italian *condottiere* (a leader of a group
of mercenaries) Facino Cane and his marauding soldiers were
widely loathed and much feared. One day a rich gentleman,
dressed in a fine doublet, complained to Cane that one of his
men had robbed him and stolen his coat. Cane asked him, "Were
you wearing that doublet on the day of the robbery?" The man
replied "Yes". Cane immediately ordered him, "Get out!"
adding "It wasn't one of my soldiers who robbed you. None of
them would have left you that doublet!"

? ! ? ! ? ! ? ! ? ! ? ! ? ! ?

FASCINATING FACTS

Last of the Greeks
Ancient Greece

Ever wondered what happened to the great
Greek civilization? After Alexander the Great
defeated Persia at the Battle of Gaugamela in
331 BC he became known as the King of Asia and
the Greek Empire became huge and very
wealthy. However, when Alexander died in
323 BC his greedy generals fought over the bits
of the empire and the army became so weakened
that it was easy for the Romans to come and
take over.

? ! ? ! ? ! ? ! ? ! ? ! ? ! ?

Charles VIII
Toward the end of the fifteenth century, Charles VIII of France
popularized men's shoes with square toes. Why? Charles hoped
to hide the fact that he had six toes on one of his feet.

Weird News Stories

SINGING SIAMESE

Siamese twins named Millie and Christina were famous singers, Millie a soprano and Christina a contralto. Born in Wilmington, North Carolina, in 1851, the twins had four legs but only one body. Either head could control the other's feet, so Millie could sing while beating time with Christina's foot, and Christina could sing while beating time with Millie's foot. They sang throughout America and Europe, and died in Wilmington in 1911, aged sixty.

Ghiyas-ud-Din Khilji, Ottoman sultan

"I have passed in ease and prosperity," the fifteenth-century Sultan Ghiyas-ud-Din Khilji declared on his deathbed, "and in a state of pleasure such has been the lot of no monarch." He wasn't kidding: the sultan had some 15,000 wives and concubines!

Christopher Columbus, Italian explorer 1451–1506

Christopher Columbus once attended an elaborate banquet, held in his honour by the grand cardinal of Spain. Though treated with deference by most of the company, he was pointedly asked by an envious courtier whether he believed that someone else would have discovered the New World had he not done so first. Columbus did not reply directly, but, taking a boiled egg in his hand, invited the guests to make it stand on its end. When everyone had tried and failed, Columbus tapped the tip of the egg against the table. Partially crushed, it was soon set standing on its flattened base. The point was clear: once Columbus had shown the way, anyone could follow.

Weird News Stories

LINCOLN'S DREAM

On an April night in 1865– with the trials of the Civil War still heavy on his mind – President Abraham Lincoln lay asleep and dreaming. In his dream, he was asleep in his huge bed in the White House. Suddenly he was wakened by sobbing. Getting up and following the sound of the weeping, Lincoln found himself in the East Room. There he saw people filing past a catafalque guarded by soldiers. The men and women were paying their last respects to a body laid in state.

The face of the corpse was covered from Lincoln's view, but he could see that those present were deeply affected by the person's death. Finally, he went to one of the soldiers and asked who was dead. "The President," was the answer. "He was killed by an assassin." With that horrifying reply came a loud outcry of grief from the group near the catafalque – and Lincoln woke up.

This troubling dream, which Lincoln told his wife Mary and several of their friends, turned out to be a prophetic one. In that very month, Lincoln went to the theatre for a rare night away from his pressing responsibilities. Awaiting him there instead of a night of pleasure was a fatal bullet from an assassin's gun.

Sir Francis Drake, English naval hero and explorer circa
1540–1596
Drake's famous exploit, namely the singeing of the King of
Spain's beard in 1588, where he destroyed thirty ships in Cadiz
harbour as the Spanish were fitting out for the invasion of
England, was carried out in the face of Queen Elizabeth's
reluctance to provoke the Spaniards. Apparently she hoped,
despite the evidence of Spain's warlike preparations, to reach a
negotiated settlement. She unwillingly gave the order to allow
Drake, who had been hanging around in Plymouth harbour for
some time, to set off on his hostile errand.

However, no sooner had she given the order than she had
second thoughts, and sent another dispatch rider to Plymouth to
countermand it. Drake however had guessed that such a second
order might be forthcoming so as soon as he received the first he
put to sea immediately. Initially the queen was very angry, but
there was nothing she could do to stop him. Queen Elizabeth's
displeasure proved to be short-lived, the Spanish Armada was
utterly destroyed and the glory of Elizabethan England assured.

Christopher Columbus, Italian explorer 1451–1506
While anchored off Jamaica in 1504, Christopher Columbus found
himself in dire straits. Though his supplies were running low, the
Jamaican Indians refused to sell him any more food. Consulting his
almanac, Columbus noticed that a lunar eclipse was due a few days
later. On the appointed day, he summoned the Jamaican leaders
and warned them that he would blot out the moon that very evening
if his demands for food were not promptly met. The Jamaicans only
laughed at him – until later that night when the eclipse began. As
the moon disappeared before their eyes, they visited Columbus in a
state of terror, whereupon he agreed to stop his magic in exchange
for food. The offer was accepted and the moon "restored."

? ! ? ! ? ! ? ! ? ! ? ! ? ! ?

! FASCINATING FACTS !

? **Loud Roman Geese** ?

Roman Empire

! !

? In 390 BC, the Gauls were trying to attack ?
Rome's Capitoline Hill. Apparently, the Romans'
holy geese made such loud squawking noises that
! the Romans woke up and so evaded capture. !

? ! ? ! ? ! ? ! ? ! ? ! ? ! ?

Grisly Tales from History

Child Labour

17th Century

During Victorian times it was
common to send children as
young as five to work, sweeping
chimneys and working down coal
mines. This left some children in
the dark for up to thirteen hours a day. In the mines the
youngest child workers were known as "trappers" which
meant that they had to be in the dark in a tiny cramped
and cold space and open or close ventilators called "traps"
to allow a little air into the mines.

Nicolas Monardes, Spanish doctor circa 1493–1588
In 1577, shortly after the introduction of tobacco from the New
World, a Spanish doctor named Nicolas Monardes published a
book entitled *Joyful News out of the New Found World* detailing
its supposed medicinal properties for the first time.

Among the conditions for which tobacco was a recommended
treatment? Headaches, arthritis, various wounds, and stomach
cramps. Moreover, it is perhaps a testament to the sorry state of
sixteenth-century oral hygiene that tobacco was aslo
recommended as a cure for toothaches – and bad breath!

Monardes's prescriptions were followed for more than 200
years.

Montezuma II circa 1466–1520
Montezuma II, the last Aztec ruler in Mexico, between 1502 and
1520, was famed for his gluttony. On a typical night he ate
chicken, turkey, songbirds, doves, ducks, rabbits, pheasants,
partridges, quail, and – according to a second-hand report – once
ate an adolescent boy or two, followed by tortillas and hot
chocolate.

Charles II, 1630–85
Arise Evans had a fungus nose. He said it had been revealed to
him that the king's hand would cure him, and at the first coming
of King Charles II into St James's Park, he kissed the king's
hand, and rubbed his nose on it. The king was greatly dismayed
but Evans was cured.

183

Weird News Stories

BURYING THE YOGI

In 1837 in Lahore, in what is today Pakistan, the yogi Haridas was buried alive for forty days. British Colonel Sir Claude Wade, Dr Janos Honiborger, and the British Consul at Lahore all solemnly corroborated that he was locked in a box, placed in a sealed pavilion with doors and windows tightly blocked shut, and guarded day and night. After forty days, the box was opened.

Haridas had not gone into the tomb unprepared. For days before his burial he had no food but milk. On the burial day itself he ate nothing, but performed dhauti – a yoga purification practice that involves swallowing a long strip of cloth, leaving it in the stomach to soak up bile and other impurities, and then withdrawing it. Haridas then did another cleansing ritual. All the openings of his body were then sealed up with wax, and his tongue was rolled back to seal the entrance to his throat. Then he was buried.

When the box was opened the yogi's assistant washed him with warm water, removed the wax, and rubbed his scalp with warm yeast. He forced his teeth open with a knife, unfolded his tongue, and massaged his body with butter. After half an hour Haridas was up and about.

Hennig Brand 1630–circa 1710

Hennig Brand was a German merchant and alchemist, noted for his discovery of phosphorus. While experimenting with urine one day in 1669, he discovered a novel compound. Despite its remarkable incendiary properties, however, Brand was very disappointed with his experimental result and virtually ignored it. Indeed, the compound was later "discovered" again by Robert Boyle (1627–1691). Why was Brand so disappointed? As a merchant and alchemist, he was seeking to restore his wealth by converting base metals into gold – and all he got was phosphorus.

Dom Perignon, French cellarmaster circa 1638–1715

One day in 1688, blind cellarmaster Dom Perignon inadvertently discovered champagne. "Oh, come quickly!" he is alleged to have cried out. "I am drinking stars!"

Philip Dormer Stanhope, Fourth Earl of Chesterfield 1694–1773

Towards the end of his life, the English politician, diplomat, and writer Lord Chesterfield became so infirm that his carriage rides were conducted at a very, very slow pace. An acquaintance once encountered the Earl on such an expedition and congratulated him on being up and about and apparently able to take the air. "I do not come out so much for the air," Chesterfield replied, "as for the benefit of rehearsing my funeral."

Grisly Tales from History

The Original Iron Maiden

19th Century

Did you know that an iron maiden is an iron cabinet allegedly built to torture or kill a person by piercing the body with sharp objects (such as knives, spikes, or nails), while he or she is forced to remain standing? The condemned bleeds profusely and is weakened slowly, eventually dying because of blood loss, or perhaps asphyxiation. In addition, the condemned were starved for a period of seven to twenty days to maximize their suffering and weakness. They were then struck on the back repeatedly with a large metal rod, stripped, then forced to walk through the streets, at which point all civilians were permitted to whip them from any angle, including the face.

The most famous device was the iron maiden of Nuremberg. The Nuremberg iron maiden was actually built in the nineteenth century as a misinterpretation of a medieval *Schandmantel* (cloak of shame), which was made of wood and tin but without spikes. The "cloak of shame" did not harm the body, but was used as a chastisement for poachers and prostitutes, who were made to wear it in public for a certain time. The iron maiden of Nuremberg was anthropomorphic. It was probably styled after Mary, the mother of Jesus, with a carved likeness of her on the face. The maiden was about 7 feet (2.1 m) tall and 3 feet (0.9 m) wide, had double doors, and was big enough to contain an adult man. Inside the tomb-sized container, the iron maiden was fitted with dozens of sharp spikes. Supposedly, they were designed so that when the doors were shut, the spikes skewered the subject, yet missed vital organs, permitting him to remain alive and upright. The spikes were also movable in order to accommodate each person.

The condemned person was kept in an extremely confined space to maximize his level of suffering by claustrophobia. Mobility was nearly impossible, and as the condemned person was weakened by the ordeal, the piercing objects would remain in place and tear into the body even further, causing even more intense pain. The doors of the maiden could be opened and closed one at a time, without giving the victim opportunity to escape. Supposedly, this was helpful when checking on the victim.

George I 1660–1727

When the Elector of Hanover became England's George I in 1714, his wife could not become the Queen of England because she had committed adultery. George had her placed under house arrest in Ahlden Castle, where she remained for thirty-two years. (Those who knew the woman's fate called her the "Prisoner of Ahlden" and she remains known as such today.) Ironically, George himself had arrived in England with his two mistresses; adultery was a crime only for women.

Louis XIV, "Le Roi Soleil" 1638–1715

Dentistry in eighteenth-century Paris was so horribly barbaric that, after having several teeth pulled by an overzealous dentist, King Louis XIV drank some soup – and had it cascade out of his *nose*!

187

SÉANCE FOR A PRESIDENT

During the presidency of Abraham Lincoln the vogue for the new Spiritualism was at its height among fashionable people. Even the President – a far from fashionable man – was drawn into it. Colonel Simon F. Kase, a lobbyist who had several times met Lincoln to discuss a railroad project with him, tells of encountering the President at a séance in the home of Mrs Laurie and daughter Mrs Miller. She was known for making a piano beat time on the floor as she played while in trance. Kase said of the occasion that Mrs Miller began to play, and the front of the piano in truth rose off the floor and beat the time of the tune with heavy thuds. Kase asked if he could sit on the instrument so that he could "verify to the world that it moved." The medium composedly answered that he and as many others as wished could sit on the piano. Four men did: Kase, a judge, and two of the soldiers who were accompanying Lincoln. Mrs Miller again began to play and the piano – heedless of its load – began to rise and thump, lifting at least four inches off the floor. Kase concluded ruefully: "It was too rough riding; we got off while the instrument beat the time until the tune was played out."

188

? ! ? ! ? ! ? ! ? ! ? ! ? ! ?

Rome vs Carthage
Roman Empire

The first Roman war with Carthage was in 264 BC and battles between the two raged for the next twenty-three years. Eventually, the Romans won and by 146 BC Rome was the greatest power in the Mediterranean.

? ! ? ! ? ! ? ! ? ! ? ! ? ! ?

John Byng, British admiral 1704–1757

When John Byng was court-martialed and brought before the firing squad (for failing to relieve the island of Minorca while under French attack), it was suggested that his face should be covered with a handkerchief, lest the sight of his sorrow breed reluctance in his executioners.

Byng announced "If it will frighten them, let it be done, they will not frighten me."

Grisly Tales from History

In the Factories

19th Century

The Industrial Revolution in the nineteenth century was a time when machines were first invented to do things that had previously been done by hand, like spinning yarn and weaving cloth. Most of the machines were originally powered by steam and were sometimes kept going all day and night so a lot of coal had to be burned to make enough steam to power them. Apparently the air became so smoky that all the surrounding buildings turned black and there was a huge increase in breathing problems due to the polluted air. Even worse, there were many accidents with people getting themselves caught in the new machines. The doctors would amputate arms and legs without any anaesthetic.

Maximilien François Marie Isidore de Robespierre 1758–1794

As a young man, Maximilien Robespierre was so opposed to the death penalty that he gave up a promising legal career rather than work in a court which sentenced prisoners to the scaffold.

Contradictorily, after assuming control of the French Revolution in 1793, Robespierre, as leader of the Jacobins, launched the Reign of Terror that sent hundreds to the guillotine. His laws permitting the confiscation of property and arrest of suspected traitors soon led to a backlash. Robespierre was arrested in 1794, and promptly met his end (ironically without a trial) on the guillotine.

Weird News Stories

WHY DOES THE SUN SHINE?

Until the 1930s, no one knew why the sun shines. It was only then that it was understood that it is a vast nuclear furnace.

Joseph Merlin 1735–1803

The first roller skates were attempted two centuries ago by Joseph Merlin. His first public demonstration ended in disaster. As a renowned maker of violins and harpsichords, the Belgian-born Merlin moved to London in 1760, where he dreamed up the idea of replacing the blades on ice skates with metal wheels. To dramatize his invention, Merlin dressed as a minstrel and made a spectacular entrance on skates at an elegant masquerade ball. He dazzled the other guests as he wheeled gracefully about the ballroom floor while playing a violin. Then, as his admirers watched in horror, Merlin lost control and sailed headlong into a crystal mirror, demolishing it and his handcrafted violin. He also reportedly broke his nose.

Georg Wilhelm Hegel, German idealist philosopher 1770–1831

Even on his deathbed Hegel remained abstractly philosophical. "Only one man ever understood me," he remarked, with a pause, "and even he didn't understand me."

191

ZOMBIE WORKERS

William Seabrook avidly studied the spirit religions of the West Indies in the 1920s. In his book *The Magic Island* he relates a strange tale told to him by a Haitian farmer. It seems that there was a bumper sugar cane crop in 1918, and labourers were in short supply. One day Joseph, an old headman, appeared leading "a band of ragged creatures who shuffled along behind him, staring dumbly, like people in a daze." They were not ordinary labourers. They were zombies – dead men whom Joseph had brought back to life by magic to slave for him in the fields.

Zombies must never taste salt according to the farmer's tale, so Joseph's wife fed them special unseasoned food. But one day she took pity on them and bought them some candy, not knowing it was made of peanuts. As soon as the zombies tasted the salty nuts, they realized they were dead. With a terrible cry they set off for their own village. Stumbling past living relatives who recognized them in horror, they "approached the graveyard . . . and rushed among the graves, and each before his own empty grave so that everyone could see that the man was truly dead."

Abbe Grioni, Venetian monk 18th Century

Even nuns and clerics were not immune from the Las Vegas-like madness of eighteenth-century Venice. Nuns wearing pearls and low-cut gowns could be seen fighting among themselves for the honour of serving as mistress to a visiting papal nuncio. One evening, in a casino in 1762, the Abbe Grioni bet all his clothes on the turn of the wheel, lost, and promptly returned to his monastery, completely naked.

Earl of Rosse, Irish astronomer 1800–1867

In 1845 the amateur astronomer, the Earl of Rosse, built a telescope with a lens six feet in diameter. Dubbed the Leviathan, it was easily the largest telescope of its day. While Rosse was applauded for his efforts, however, the results he achieved were less than stellar. The problem? He built it in Ireland, where the weather was so bad he could hardly ever use it.

Karl Friedrich Gauss 1777–1855

The famous nineteenth-century mathematician Karl Friedrich Gauss once proposed that ten-mile strips of trees delineating the Pythagorean Theorem should be planted in the Siberian steppes – so that they might be visible to alien beings on other planets. In 1840, the Austrian Joseph Johann von Littrow recommended setting immense geometrical fires in the Sahara for the same purpose. So far no aliens have acknowledged these structures.

193

MAN UNDER TRAIN

It was November 1971 in London on a day like any other. In one of the city's underground stations, a train was approaching the platform. Suddenly a young man hurled himself directly into the path of the moving train. The horrified driver slammed on the brakes, certain that there was no way to stop the train before the man was crushed under the wheels. But miraculously the train did stop. The first carriage had to be jacked up to remove the badly injured man, but the wheels had not passed over him and he survived.

The young man turned out to be a gifted architect who was recovering from a nervous breakdown. His amazing rescue from death was based on coincidence. For the investigation of the accident revealed that the train had not stopped because of the driver's hasty braking. Seconds before, acting on an impulse and completely unaware of the man about to throw himself on the tracks, a passenger had pulled down the emergency handle, which automatically applies the brakes of the train. The passenger had no particular reason for doing so. In fact, the Transport Authority considered prosecuting him on the grounds that he had had no reasonable cause for using the emergency system!

194

Robert Owen 1771–1858

At the height of the Industrial Revolution in the nineteenth century, child labour was prevalent in England's factories and coal mines. One day Robert Owen, the famed industrialist (and utopian socialist) encountered a twelve-year-old breaker boy, exhausted from separating shale from coal, completely covered in toxic black coal dust.

"Do you know God?" Owen asked him. "No," the boy replied. "He must work in some other mine."

Ferdinand I, Austrian emperor 1793–1875

Ferdinand I of Austria suffered from such severe bouts of insanity that, during his reign, a council managed affairs of state. Unsurprisingly, this untenable state of affairs ended in revolution and Ferdinand was forced to abdicate in favor of his nephew, Francis Joseph. According to historian A. J. P. Taylor, among the most lucid utterances of his entire reign was, "I am the emperor . . . and I want dumplings!"

Grisly Tales from History

The Great Stink

19th Century

In 1886 the River Thames got so filled with sewage and rubbish that MPs had to leave the Houses of Parliament because the stench was so bad. People were still quite ignorant about hygiene and outbreaks of cholera and typhoid were common and widespread.

John Spencer-Churchill, Tenth Duke of Marlborough
1897–1972

The Duke of Marlborough, who lived in considerable style at Blenheim Palace, once visited one of his daughters in her relatively modest home.

Early one morning, she was astonished to hear her father hollering down the stairs, complaining that his toothbrush was "not working": it was not foaming as it should, the duke explained, angrily demanding a replacement.

Marlborough's daughter was obliged to explain that foam was produced only when "toothpaste" was applied to the brush – a task usually performed by the duke's valet.

Weird News Stories

LOST IN SPACE

In 1952 Ronald Reagan was in Brazil at a political function and, towards the end of the meal, he was asked to make a speech.

"Now would you join me in a toast to President Figueiredo," he said, "and to all the people of Bolivia . . . oh no, that's wrong, that's where I'm going next . . . erm . . . to the people of Brazil, yes that's right, Brazil." His voice trailed off as one of his aides drew his attention to the fact that his next destination was in fact Bogota, the capital of Colombia.

Josef Victor von Scheffel, German writer 1826–1886
One summer day, the young Josef Scheffel set out on a hiking
trip along the right bank of the Rhine. The day grew unbearably
hot so Scheffel removed his clothes in a secluded spot and dived
in for a swim. Having grievously underestimated the river's
current, however, he barely managed to regain the shore – on
the opposite (left) bank. Entirely naked, the young poet was
obliged to seek assistance at the nearest inn, where he soon
found himself being questioned by the district military
policeman, who also happened to be visiting: "Where did you
come from?" the officer demanded.

"From the opposite bank, Sir," Scheffel replied.

"And what's your name?"

"I'm the writer, Josef Victor von Scheffel."

"Indeed?" the officer cried, "Show me your papers!"

Count Maurice Maeterlinck 1862–1949, **Belgian poet and
dramatist, winner of the Nobel Prize for Literature** 1911
Despite its lack of modern amenities, the Belgian writer Maurice
Maeterlinck once graciously accepted an invitation to visit a
French chateau the remote location of which would enable him
to relax and write in peace.

Having arrived while his hostess was away, Maeterlinck
asked the maid to direct him to the washroom. She led him
down a corridor, at the end of which stood an immense,
apparently solid oak throne – from behind which she retrieved a
large cloak and face mask. "Here you are, monsieur," she said.
"You wear these so no one knows who is sitting here."

Maeterlinck politely thanked the woman and was miles from
the chateau by the time his hostess had returned.

Weird News Stories

PIGGING OUT

Detective Constable Bernard Startup, of Linden Avenue, Oldham, was disturbed at 9.30 pm on 5 August 1972 by a knock at his door. The man on his step alerted DC Startup to the fact that a huge hairy pig was eating the young fir trees in his garden. As the pair watched, the alarming animal stretched too far in search of food and fell into the fish pond. While it was thus distracted, Startup blocked off the entrance to his garden with his car, and phoned his colleagues. The animal was eventually tranquillized by a vet. This oddity became a mystery when it was discovered that the 200-lb beast was a wild boar, a species supposedly extinct in Britain for 400 years. The animal was taken to Marwell Zoological Park when no collector or zoo claimed it as their own. *Aldershot News*, UK

John Harvey Kellogg, American physician and social reformer 1852–1943

Doctor John Harvey Kellogg prescribed daily yoghurt enemas to patients at his Battle Creek, Michigan sanitarium. He also invented breakfast cereal. Both corn flakes and Graham crackers were designed to inhibit masturbation, based on the notion that bland food and self-abuse were somehow incompatible.

Hollywood Mobster

20th Century

In the early twentieth century a
mobster known as Benjamin
"Bugsy" Siegel charmed most
everyone that he met, especially in Hollywood, killing for
the Mob at the same time as seducing nubile young
starlets. Although sent to California to watch over the
Mob's interests, many believed that what he really wanted
in Hollywood was to be an actor. This dead mobster has
long been said to be haunting two places that he knew in
life . . . one of them, a place that he loved, and the other, a
spot where he had left a terrified presence behind.

He grew up on New York's Lower East Side and by the
age of fourteen, was already running his own criminal gang.
He formed an early alliance with a youth named Meyer
Lansky, who was already a criminal genius in his teens. By
1920, they had formed a gang specializing in bootleg liquor,
gambling, and auto theft. The emerging national crime syndicate assigned Spiegel to carry out numerous murders that
were aimed at gaining control of various criminal operations.
He became an excellent killer and was so excited by it that
he was said to be "bugs", or mad, and was called "Bugsy" as
a result – though never to his face.

In the 1930s Siegel was sent to California to run the
syndicate's West Coast operations, including the lucrative
racing wire service for bookmakers and a casino club
called the Flamingo Hotel. He was suave and entertaining
and became friends with Hollywood celebrities like Jean

Harlow, George Raft, Clark Gable, Gary Cooper and Cary Grant. Many of them even put money into his enterprises. A times he was the life and soul of any party; at other times, he was a cold-blooded killer. On occasion, Siegel could be at a party with his "high class friends" and then slip away for a gangland execution, all in the same night. The syndicate became upset about the $6 million they had invested, as the Flamingo, when it opened, was a financial disaster. Reportedly, the Mob demanded that Siegel make good on their investment, but what they didn't know was that Bugsy had also been skimming from the construction funds and from the gambling profits. Virginia Hill had been busy hiding the money in Swiss bank accounts.The syndicate passed a death sentence on Siegel at the famous Havana conference in December 1946. On 20 June 1947, Siegel was sitting in the living room of Virginia Hill's Beverly Hills mansion. She was away in Europe at the time. He was reading the newspaper when two steel-jacketed slugs tore through the front window. One of them shattered the bridge of his nose and exited through his left eye, while the other entered his right cheek and blew out the back of his neck. Authorities later found his right eye on the dining room floor, more than 15 feet from his body. Bugsy Siegel was dead before he hit the floor.

Virginia Hill's former home is reportedly still haunted by the panicking presence of Bugsy Siegel as he scrambled for cover from the bullets that killed him. According to reports, witnesses have been surprised for years by the apparition of a man running and ducking across the living room of the house, only to disappear as suddenly as it had appeared. After Siegel was assassinated, the mob continued to support the Flamingo Hotel and eventually saw it grow and prosper. And it is at the Flamingo where the spirit of Bugsy Siegel is said to reside today.

He is believed to haunt the Presidential Suite of the hotel, where he lived for many years. Guests in this room have apparently reported a number of strange encounters with his ghost, from eerie, moving cold spots to items that vanish and move about the suite. They have also seen him in the bathroom and near the pool table. Those who have supposedly seen him say his spirit doesn't seem unhappy or distressed. They report him as seeming very content.

William Randolph Hearst 1863–1951

The American newspaper and magazine publisher and art collector, William Randolph Hearst, always in search of sensational stories, once sent a telegram to a leading astronomer asking, "Is there life on Mars? Please cable 1,000 words." The astronomer replied, "Nobody knows," and repeated it 500 times.

Hermann Bahr, Austrian playwright, author, and theatre director 1863–1934

A young poet once sent Hermann Bahr an historical tragedy, along with a request for his opinion: "If you find any faults, please be honest with me. Words of criticism from such a source would make me feel ennobled." Bahr returned the manuscript with this comment: "I'd like to make you at least an archduke."

201

Stanley Baldwin, British prime minister 1876–1947
Winston Churchill once pilloried one of Prime Minister Stanley
Baldwin's policies in the House of Commons. "History will say
that the right honorable gentleman was wrong in this matter,"
Churchill bluntly declared. "I know it will, because I shall write
the history."

**Winston Leonard Spenser Churchill, British politician and
writer,** prime minister from 1940, 1874–1965
Shortly after Harold Macmillan was chosen as the new
Conservative leader (over Rab Butler), a private secretary
entered Churchill's office and found him muttering: "Intelligent,
yes. Good-looking, yes. Well-meaning, yes, but not the stuff of
which prime ministers are made."
    "But would Rab have been any better?" the secretary
interjected.
    "I was thinking," Churchill replied, "of Melbourne."
(Churchill often spoke of such historical figures as Walter
Raleigh and Henry VIII as though they were his contemporaries;
Lord Melbourne had died in 1848.)

GET THAT MAN

Until 1990 prison inmates in Texas were used as bait for training attack dogs. The practice was only halted after six injured prisoners sued the state. During an investigation, it emerged that the Vice-Chairman of the Texas Board of Criminal Justice was one of the dog-handlers. So enthusiastic was the VC about his "hobby" that he even had jackets printed for himself and his fellow trainers featuring the slogan: "The Ultimate Hunt". *LA Times*, USA

Robert Hutchings Goddard, American physicist and inventor 1882–1945

In 1921, a curious editorial appeared in the *New York Times* critiquing the revolutionary work of rocket scientist Robert Goddard:

"Professor Goddard does not know the relation between action and reaction and the need to have something better than a vacuum against which to react," it declared. "He seems to lack the basic knowledge ladled out daily in high schools."

Goddard knew the *Times* was wrong. He had used airtight chambers to show that a rocket could indeed fly in a vacuum, thanks to Newton's third law. Sure enough, after the Apollo 11 mission in 1969, the *Times* published a retraction: "Further investigation and experimentation have confirmed the findings of Isaac Newton in the seventeenth century, and it is now definitely established that a rocket can function in a vacuum as well as in an atmosphere. The *Times* regrets the error."

Laszlo Biro, Hungarian inventor, noted for his invention of the ballpoint pen 1899–1985

While working as a journalist in the early part of the twentieth century, Hungarian-born Laszlo Biro was often annoyed by fountain pens. He began to wonder whether the troublesome object could be replaced with something more convenient. The result was the "biro" (ballpoint pen). The commercial version of Laszlo's invention was launched in Argentina. Ironically, however, Biro neglected to use his invention to file for North American patents and, as a result, lost what would have amounted to a sizeable fortune.

Laurence Olivier, British actor 1907–1989

Although Laurence Olivier, often named the finest actor of the twentieth century, was often asked for advice from aspiring performers, he categorically refused to oblige . . . with one exception. The extent of Olivier's advice to his fellow thespians was to, "Relax your feet."

Though he was knighted in 1947 and made a life peer in 1970, Olivier remained a humble man – refusing to carry on a conversation with anyone who would not address him simply as "Larry".

Ford Madox Ford, born Ford Hermann Hueffer, American writer and editor 1873–1939

The turn of the twentieth century marked the height of oddball treatments for neurasthenia, hysteria, and other newly named neurological disorders. Ford Madox Ford, never one to stint himself, saw nineteen specialists between 1903 and 1906 and underwent treatments which ranged from being fed one grape every quarter of an hour for sixteen hours out of the day to having indecent photographs of a singular banality flashed before his eyes.

Virginia Woolf, British novelist 1882–1941

In the twentieth century, literary people seemed particularly susceptible both to nervous breakdowns and the quacks who treated them. Viginia Woolf famously saw five different doctors and underwent the so-called Weir Mitchell cure, from which she later extracted a measure of revenge by mocking the doctor in *Mrs Dalloway*.

Waterboarding in the USA

21st Century

A twenty-first century form of torture is waterboarding. Waterboarding consists of immobilizing an individual and pouring water over his face to simulate drowning, which produces a severe gag reflex, making the subject believe his death is imminent while ideally not causing permanent physical damage. "The threat of imminent death" is one of the legal definitions of torture under US law. Depending on the exact set-up, the water may or may not actually get into the person's mouth and nose; but the physical experience of being underneath a wave of water seems to be secondary to the psychological experience. The person's mind believes he is drowning, and his gag reflex kicks in as if he were choking on all that water falling on his face. It is used to obtain information, coerce confessions, and for punishment and intimidation.

The practice garnered renewed attention and notoriety in September 2006 when further reports charged that the Bush administration had authorized its use in the interrogations of US "War on Terror" detainees. Though the Bush administration has never formally acknowledged its use, Vice President Dick Cheney told an interviewer that he did not believe "a dunk in water" to be a form of torture but rather a "very important tool" for use in interrogations

The UN Convention against Torture prohibits the intentional infliction of severe pain or suffering In November 2005, anonymous sources told ABC news that the US Central Intelligence Agency uses waterboarding, but does not deem it torture.

Dick Tuck, American practical joker 1924–

Dick Tuck (whose business card once featured a mock
dictionary entry for "political prank") was the twentieth
century's premiere political practical joker. Tuck pulled off his
best-known prank in Los Angeles in 1962, during Nixon's
Californian gubernatorial campaign. The press reported that five
years earlier Howard Hughes had lent the candidate's brother
two hundred and five thousand dollars. The loan, which had not
been repaid, was widely seen as an attempt by Hughes to curry
favour with Nixon. At a rally in Chinatown, Tuck distributed
signs and fortune cookies that read "Welcome Nixon!" over a
row of Chinese characters. Nixon smiled broadly for the
cameras, until he was informed that the Chinese script said,
"How about the Hughes loan?" Nixon grabbed a sign and, on
camera, ripped it up.

 Later, Tuck learned, to his chagrin that the Chinese characters
actually spelled out "What about the huge loan?"

Woody Allen, born Allan Stewart Konigsberg 1935–

In the middle of the twentieth century, Los Angeles was
considered by many New Yorkers to be little short of a cultural
wasteland. H. L. Mencken had called it "Moronia", Aldous
Huxley had commented that "thought is barred in this city of
Dreadful Joy and conversation is unknown". Woody Allen was
to remark that the city"s only contribution to culture was the
practice of turning right at a red light, made legal in the 1947
vehicle code."

? ! ? ! ? ! ? ! ? ! ? ! ? ! ?

FASCINATING FACTS

The Nazca Plain
100 BC—AD 60

In Peru, between the Andes and the Pacific, lies the
Nazca Plain. It is a vast, flat expanse of sunbaked stones;
and, at ground level at least, extremely boring. Fly over
it, however, and what had seemed like abstract markings
from ground level resolve themselves into complex
drawings of a bird, a lizard, a monkey, a spider and many
other stylized images. They were created by moving the
dark stones that litter the surface of the desert to
reveal the lighter earth beneath. This has been done on a
grand scale, some of the "drawings" are over a hundred
feet long.

These markings are believed to have been made by the
Nazcan Indians, a pre-Inca race, between 100 BC and AD
600. It has been suggested that they correspond to
some astronomical alignment, but study has shown that
the small extent to which they do could very easily be
coincidental. Erich von Däniken, the God-as-Astronaut
theorist, believes the lines to be landing strips from alien
spacecraft. In his book *Chariots of the Gods?* he shows
two parallel lines with a widened area halfway along one
of them. This, he puts forward, is a runway with a flying
saucer parking area. The picture is in fact one of the
Nazcan birds' legs. The wide area is its knee, a space
hardly large enough to park a bicycle in.

Von Däniken does raise an interesting question
however. Short of building hot-air balloons, the Nazcan
Indians could never have been sure that they looked as
they intended. One can only conclude that the pictures
were designed to be seen by the gods. Whether these
gods drove spaceships or not is a matter for conjecture.

? ! ? ! ? ! ? ! ? ! ? ! ? ! ?

Weird News Stories

LOVING SNAKES

An Arizona man decided to demonstrate his courage to his friends by kissing a rattlesnake that they had come across in the wild. The man picked up the snake and planted a kiss on its "lips"; unsurprisingly, he was bitten – on the tongue – by the shocked beast. In an effort to remove the venom, the man tried a drastic and unorthodox method. He attached his tongue to the battery of his car.   *Arizona Republic*, USA

Sigmund Freud, the father of psychoanalysis 1856–1939
Sigmund Freud was not without his critics. Among them was Dr Sophie Freud, Sigmund's own granddaughter. "In my eyes," she once remarked, "both Adolf Hitler and Sigmund Freud were false prophets of the twentieth century."

Weird News Stories

DOGGIE BAG

A department store in Japan will, for the equivalent of about £50, prepare a gourmet carry-out meal for your pet dog. A popular menu consists of premium rare beef, unsalted ham, sausages, cheese, and white chocolate for dessert.

Wall Street Journal, USA

WEIRD TALES

The Mystery of Eilean More – The Island of Disappearing Men

In the empty Atlantic, seventeen miles to the west of the Hebrides, lie the Flannan Islands, known to seafarers as the Seven Hunters. The largest and most northerly of these is called Eilean More – which means in fact "big island". Like the *Mary Celeste*, its name has become synonymous with an apparently insoluble mystery of the sea. These bleak islands received their name from a seventh-century bishop, St Flannan, who built a small chapel on Eilean More. Hebridean shepherds often ferried their sheep over to the islands to graze on the rich turf; but they themselves would never spend a night there, for the islands are supposed to be haunted by spirits and by "little folk".

In the last decades of the nineteenth century, as Britain's sea trade increased, many ships sailing north or south from Clydebank were wrecked on the Flannans, and in 1895 the Northern Lighthouse Board announced that a lighthouse would be built on Eilean More. They expected construction to take two years; but rough seas, and the problems of hoisting stones and girders up a 200-foot cliff, made it impossible to stick to the schedule; Eilean More lighthouse was finally opened in December 1899. For the next year its beam could be seen reflected on the rough seas between Lewis and the Flannans. Then, eleven days before Christmas 1900, the light went out.

A steamer was sent to investigate. There were three men on Eilean More responsible for keeping the lighthouse alight – James Ducat, Donald McArthur, and Thomas Marshall. On Boxing Day 1900, the Hesperus left harbour soon after daylight, its skipper a man called Joseph Moore. The swell was still heavy, and the Hesperus had to make three approaches before she was able to moor by the eastern jetty. No flags had answered their signals, and there was no sign of life. Moore was the first to reach the entrance gate. It was closed. He cupped his hands and shouted, then hurried up the steep path. The main door was closed, and no one answered his shouts. Like the Mary Celeste, the lighthouse was empty. In the main room the clock had stopped, and the ashes in the fireplace were cold. In the sleeping quarters upstairs – Moore waited until he was joined by two seamen before he ventured upstairs, afraid of what he might find there – the beds were neatly made, and the place was tidy.

James Ducat, the chief keeper, had kept records on a slate. The last entry was for 15 December at 9 am, the day the light went out. But this had not been for lack of oil; the wicks were trimmed and the lights all ready to be lit. Everything was in order. So it was clear that the men had completed their basic duties for the day before tragedy struck them; when evening came there had been no one on the island to light the lamp. But 15 December had been a calm day . . .

Two days later investigators landed on Eilean More, and tried to reconstruct what had happened. At first it looked as if the solution was quite straightforward. On the westward jetty there was evidence of gale damage; a number of ropes were entangled round a crane which was sixty-five feet above sea-level. A tool chest kept in a crevice forty-five feet above this was missing. It looked as if a hundred-foot wave had crashed in from the Atlantic and swept it away, as well as the three men.

The fact that the oilskins belonging to Ducat and Marshall were missing seemed to support this theory; they only wore them to visit the jetties. So the investigators had a plausible theory. The two men had feared that the crane was damaged in the storm; they had struggled to the jetty in their oilskins, then been caught by a sudden huge wave . . . But in that case, what had happened to the third man, Donald McArthur, whose oilskins were still in the lighthouse? Had he perhaps rushed out to try to save them and been swept away himself?

All these theories came crashing down when someone pointed out that 15 December had been a calm day; the storms had not started until the following day. Then perhaps Ducat had simply entered the wrong date by mistake? That theory had to be abandoned when a ship's crew announced that they had passed close to the islands on the night of 15 December and that the light was already out . . .

If the three men had been on the jetty on a calm morning – it would explain why McArthur was not wearing his oilskins. Perhaps one of them had slipped into the water? Perhaps the other two had jumped in after him and been drowned. But then there were ropes and lifebelts on the jetty – why should men leap into the water when they had only to throw in a lifebelt?

In 1947 a Scottish journalist named Iain Campbell visited Eilean More on a calm day, and was standing near the west landing when the sea suddenly gave a heave, and rose seventy feet over the jetty. Then, after about a minute, it subsided back to normal. It could have been some freak of the tides, or possibly an underwater earthquake. Campbell was convinced that anyone on the jetty at that time would have been sucked into the sea. The lighthouse keeper told him that this curious "upheaval" occurs periodically, and that several men had almost been dragged into the sea.

But it is still hard to understand how three men could be involved in such an accident. Since McArthur was not wearing his oilskins, we can presume he was in the tower when it happened – if it happened. Even if his companions were swept away, would he be stupid enough to rush down to the jetty and fling himself into the sea? Only one thing is clear: that on that calm December day at the turn of the century, some accident snatched three men off Eilean More, and left not even a shred of a clue to the mystery.

ARMS TRADE

British troops participating in the recent UN actions in the Gulf were forced to wear thick, green camouflage uniforms, obviously unsuited to the desert environment. This was because four years before the British government had sold all the army's desert uniforms to Iraq.   *LA Times*, USA

Chapter Fourteen

A Brief, Unreliable History of . . .
Rock and Roll

Rock and Roll

Everything you ever wanted to know about the music that changed the world.

1

DJ Alan Freed was the first to use the term rock and roll to describe the increasingly raucous vein of R&B that was being played. The terms "rocking" and "rolling" had been increasingly used as a double entendre for dancing and sex, allowing singers to get away with some quite filthy lyrics under the pretence they were singing about dancing.

2

There is an endless and very tedious dispute about what was the very first rock and roll record. Candidates include Roy Brown's *Good Rockin' Tonite* and Big Joe Turner's *Shake, Rattle and Roll*. The Boswell Sisters actually recorded the song "Rock and Roll", in 1934, but they were singing about the motion of ocean waves, so they don't count. As the man says, if it ain't about sex, it ain't rock and roll . . .

3

One breakthrough was Bo Diddley's eponymous Bo Diddley, which was notable for the fiddly guitar beat and the fact that the drummer decided to hit the drums really, really hard.

4

Everything changed when Elvis came on the scene. He could do a great impression of the R&B singers who came before him, but had the PR advantage of being white. He had swivelly hips, a pretty face, and a weird gurgly voice. The world swooned, he joined the army, did the 1968 special dressed in leather, then got fat, and died.

5

The Beatles emerged from Liverpool via Hamburg in the early sixties. Playing a mix of urgent rock and roll and sweet pop and ballads, they became global stars. Because of them and Bob Dylan (who defected from the folkie movement to become an electric musician) it now became fashionable for singers to sing their own songs, rather than using professional songwriters, which led to some truly terrible songs being performed in the 1960s and beyond.

6

In 1962, The Rolling Stones played their first gig, playing a derivative blues-based form of rock and roll, fronted by Mick Jagger who put on a weird half-black, half-cockney accent to cover up his middle class roots. Forty-five years later they are still touring and still getting away with it.

7

The greatest rock songwriter of all time was probably Brian Wilson. He managed to force the Beach Boys, a naff family surf harmony band into recording *Good Vibrations* and *Pet Sounds*, two of the finest records ever made. Unfortunately the effort left him in a precarious mental state and after attempting to record *Smile* (during the sessions for which he was often to be found playing piano in a sandpit or wearing a toy fireman's helmet), he withdrew from public life. One of the great miracles of rock music is that he came back thirty-five years later and managed to finish *Smile*.

8

In the 1970s, rock music became a bit preposterous. Two of the absolute low points were Rick Wakeman's performance of a prog rock *King Arthur on Ice*, and Deep Purple's *Concerto for Group and Orchestra*, a title that tells its own tale of pomposity and absurdity.

9

Punk in 1976–77 promised to blow away all the pomposity of the rock dinosaurs. Everyone shouted a lot, the Sex Pistols swore on TV and then it was all over. The rock dinosaurs were replaced in the chart by electro pop and the new romantics, which wasn't quite what the punks had been hoping for.

10

Kurt Cobain was the fusion of punk spirit with rock attitude.
Forty years after Bo Diddley's drummer had hit the drums really
hard, Nirvana came up with the next evolutionary step in rock.
The drummer hit the drums really quietly in the verse, and then
really loud in the chorus. Brilliant! They were probably the last
great rock band, but we can always hope that there is more to
come.

Future Bingo

The future history of the world is hard to predict. But as we look forward in fear and hope, why not have some fun while we're waiting?

Keep this **Future Bingo** sheet to hand, and cross off any events that actually happen in the future. If you get a full page of amazing future events, then shout out "House".

If you send the finished page to the **Future Bingo** corporation (at an address yet to be determined), you may even receive a mystery prize . . .

Riots in Manila after midget elephants stampede.	I shot JFK, admits Norwegian nun.
Jedi becomes official world religion.	First shopping mall on Mars opens.
Dancing bears hold up Hollywood bank.	Jim Morrison found working in Mongolian kayaking resort.

Chapter Fifteen

Messiahs, Fanatics, and Cults

Was Jesus a Messiah?

The answer to that question may seem obvious, for his followers
certainly regarded him as *the* Messiah. But did Jesus agree with
them? The answer is probably not.

When his disciple Peter told him: "They call you the Christ,
the Messiah," Jesus advised him to be silent. The claim
obviously embarrassed him. The Jewish craving for a messiah
arose out of the longing for someone to lead them to victory.
After the Assyrian invasion, the Jews became a conquered
people, oppressed by a series of more powerful nations: the
Seleucids (descendants of Alexander the Great), the
Babylonians, the Egyptians, the Romans. For the same reason,
the British of a thousand years later came to believe firmly that
King Arthur would return to throw off the foreign yoke. Jesus
had no desire to be regarded as a military commander, which is
what the word messiah originally implied.

Jesus was only one of many Hebrew prophets who were
believed to be the messiah; the historian Josephus mentions
several of them. He regarded them all as charlatans and
agitators. Christians later changed Josephus's text, in which
Jesus is described as a small man with a hunched back and a
half-bald head, to read: "six feet tall, well grown, with a
venerable face, handsome nose . . . curly hair the colour of
unripe hazel nuts . . .", along with various other details that
transform the unprepossessing little man into the early Christian
equivalent of a film star.

But if Jesus declined to be regarded as a military leader, why
did anyone pay any attention to him? The answer is that he
announced that the end of the world was about to take place, and
that this would happen *within the lifetime of people then alive.*
This is why he told them to take no thought for the morrow, and
that God would provide. The world would soon be ending.

It was the Jews, not their Roman conquerors, who disliked Jesus. The Sadducees, who loved Greek culture and disbelieved in life after death, thought him an uncultivated fanatic. The Pharisees, who regarded themselves as the guardians of the Law, reacted angrily to Jesus's attacks on them as narrow-minded and old-fashioned. The Zealots wanted to see the Romans conquered and thrown out of Palestine, and had no patience with a messiah who preached peace and love.

While Jesus was wandering around the countryside preaching in the open air, no one worried about him. But when he rode into Jerusalem on a donkey (fulfilling the prophecy of Isaiah) and was greeted with enthusiasm by the people, the Jewish establishment became alarmed. And when Jesus threw the money changers out of the temple, they saw the writing on the wall and had him arrested. The arrest had to take place in a garden at night to avoid causing trouble.

The Jews demanded Jesus's execution, declining to allow him to be pardoned in honour of Passover. Jesus died, like so many other messiahs and political agitators, by crucifixion.

How, then, did Christianity go on to conquer the world? The answer lies partly in the many stories of miracles that circulated about Jesus – including the story that he had risen from the dead. A Jewish sect called the Messianists (or Nasoraeans) believed that Jesus would return and lead them against the Romans. At this point, a convert to Christianity named Paul produced a strange and mystical new version of Jesus's teaching that seemed to have very little to do with anything Jesus had actually said. Paul declared that Jesus was the Son of God (which Jesus had denied) who had been sent to redeem Man from the sin of Adam, and that anyone who believed in Jesus was "saved". In fact, Jesus had preached salvation through the efforts of the individual, and insisted that the Kingdom of God is within everybody. But since there was still a widespread belief that the End of the World would occur within a year or so, Paul's version of the Christian message was a powerful incentive to belief.

The Messianists regarded such a notion as absurd and blasphemous, and since they were politically stronger than Paul's Christians, it looked as if their version would triumph.

However, as it happened, the Messianists were among those wiped out by Titus, the son of the Roman emperor Vespasian, who was sent to put down the latest rebellion. He did more than that; he destroyed the Temple and carried its treasures back to Rome. Paul's "Christians" were so widely scattered that they were relatively immune from massacre. And so, by an historical accident, Paul's version of Christianity became the official version, and the "vicarious atonement" – the notion that Jesus died on the cross to redeem man from the sin of Adam – became the basis of the religion that went on to conquer the world.

By the year AD 100 it was obvious that the world was not going to end within the lifetime of Jesus's contemporaries, and that Jesus, like so many other messiahs, had quite simply been wrong. But by that time, Christianity was too powerful to die out. It was now a political force, the focus of all the dissatisfaction of the underdogs and victims of Roman brutality. The belief now spread that the end of the world would occur in the year AD 1000. And, as we have seen, there was so much violence, pestilence and bloodshed around that time that the believers had no doubt that the end was just around the corner.

FUSSY EATERS

The US Army has regulations concerning almost all aspects of a soldier's life. Here are some extracts from those regarding the baking of cookies: "They shall be wholly intact, free from chips or cracks . . . The cookies shall be tender and crisp, with an appetizing flavor, free from burnt or scorched flavor . . . They shall have been uniformly well baked with a color ranging from not lighter than chip 27885, or darker than chip 13711 . . . The color comparison shall be made under sky daylight with objects held in such a way as to avoid specular reaction."   *Ann Arbor News*, USA

The Pyramids

Some groups believe that the Great Pyramid in Egypt had encoded within its measurements many great truths. Christian sects have maintained that it was not the Egyptians who built it at all but the Israelites. According to this theory the internal passageways of the Pyramid, measured in the correct units, are a three-dimensional model of the history of the world up to Christ's birth. On a more secular level, twice the length of the base of the Pyramid divided by its height, again in the correct units, is supposed to approximate to *pi*. It is difficult to verify these statements as the nature of the correct units is a matter of conjecture, and the actual size of the Pyramid in any units is still problematic.

The Anglo-Israelite fundamentalist sect took the argument a

stage further. Not only was the Pyramid not built by the Egyptians, it was also not entirely correct to say the Israelites built it. According to the Anglo-Israelites, the Anglo-Saxon races of Britain and America were the only true tribe of Israel remaining. It was they who had built the Pyramid, as a warning that the world would end and that Christ would return on 20 August 1953. When the date passed without significant upheaval, the Anglo-Israelites began to formulate the theory that the message of the Pyramid was not literal, but a religious metaphor.

AD 132 Simon Bar Kochba

Even before the millennium, there were plenty of messiahs. In AD 132, a Jewish revolutionary named Simon Bar Kochba led a revolt against the Romans in Judaea when he learned that the Emperor Hadrian intended to build a temple dedicated to Jupiter on the site of the temple that had been destroyed by Titus. A celebrated student of the Talmud (the Jewish book of law), Rabbi Akiva, told Simon Bar Kochba: "You are the messiah." And Bar Kochba behaved exactly as a Jewish Messiah was expected to behave (and as Jesus had failed to behave); he seized towns and villages from the Romans, had his own head stamped on the coinage, and built fortresses. But he stood no real chance against the Romans, with their highly trained troops.

It took Julius Severus three-and-a-half years to destroy the rebels, and in that time he destroyed fifty fortresses and 985 villages, and killed over half a million people. Since Bar Kochba's men were guerrillas, and guerrillas survive by being supported by sympathizers, Severus set out to kill all the sympathizers. He finlly killed Bar Kochba himself in the fortress of Bethar, and renamed Jerusalem Aelia Capitolana. So one more messiah was proved to be mortal and fallible after all. The Jews were so shattered by this defeat that there were no more Jewish messiahs for many centuries.

BEAM ME UP

In late 1977 the play-offs to determine who would play Anatoly Karpov in the Chess Championship of the World were taking place between Victor Korchnoi and Boris Spassky. After having lost three games in ten days, Korchnoi made an extraordinary claim. In front of the world's media, he alleged that the KGB were beaming microwaves at him while he was thinking about his moves, to confuse his thought and affect his play. He supported his claim by pointing out that Spassky got up and left the stage after each of his moves, evidently to get out of range.

Daily Mail, UK

Moses of Crete

In about AD 435, an unnamed messiah from Crete, who called himself Moses, announced that, like his predecessor, he would lead his followers back to the Promised Land, causing the sea to part for them so they could walk on the bottom. Hundreds of followers gathered on the seashore, and Moses raised his arms and ordered the sea to separate. Then he shouted the order to march into the waves. They obeyed him, but the sea ignored his order, and many of his followers were drowned. Moses may have been drowned with them; at all events, he disappeared.

The Christ of Gevaudon

In AD 591, an unnamed messiah began to wander around France.
This man had apparently had a nervous breakdown after being
surrounded by a swarm of flies in a forest. He recovered after
two years and became a preacher, clad himself in animal skins,
and wandered down through Arles to the district of Gevaudon in
the Cevennes (noted later for a famous case of a werewolf). He
declared he was Christ, had a companion called Mary, and
healed the sick by touching them. His followers were mostly the
very poor, and they often waylaid travellers (most of whom
would be rich) and seized their money. The messiah
redistributed it to the poor. His army of 3,000 became so
powerful that most towns lost no time in acknowledging him as
the Christ.

Weird News Stories

FALSE TEETH

Police investigating strange cries
in the night coming from the
cemetery of St Mary's Church,
Felling, Durham, found a full set
of clothes and a pair of false
teeth, but no sign of the owner. A
senior officer commented: "There
are no reports of anyone looking
suspiciously undressed."   *Daily Mirror*, UK

Aldebert

In AD 742, a messiah called Aldebert, who came from Soissons, announced that he was a saint; his followers built chapels for him which he named after himself. He claimed to own a letter from Jesus himself. Pope Zachary was so worried about "Saint" Aldebert's influence that he tried hard to capture him, and, when that failed, excommunicated him. Aldebert went on for at least two more years, and seems to have died of natural causes.

Eudo de Stella

In the twelfth century another messiah called Eon or Eudo de Stella was less lucky. He gathered hordes of disciples in Brittany, and organized his followers into a Church with archbishops and bishops. Unlike Jesus of Nazareth, he had no hesitation in declaring that he was the son of God. 1144 was a good year for a messiah to acquire followers, for an appalling winter caused multitudes to starve. Eon's followers lived in the forest, and ravaged the countryside, living mainly by plunder. But in 1148, he was taken prisoner by soldiers of the Archbishop of Rouen and imprisoned in a tower, where he was starved to death. His followers refused to renounce him, and the "bishops" and "archbishops" were burned alive in the now traditional Christian spirit.

Weird News Stories

A FERTILE MULE

According to *Encyclopedia Britannica*, mules – the offspring of a horse and a donkey – are sterile. In the 1930s, Old Beck, a mule owned by the Texas Agricultural and Mechanical College proved this wrong by giving birth to two offspring, one sired by a donkey, one by a horse.

Tanchelm

One of the most remarkable messiahs of the twelfth century, Tanchelm of Antwerp, was already dead by then. He seems to have started his career as a monk, then become a diplomat working for Count Robert of Flanders, trying to persuade the Pope to hand over some of Utrecht to Count Robert. The Pope refused, and when Count Robert died, Tanchelm's career as a diplomat came to an end. He became a wandering preacher, making his headquarters in Antwerp.

Tanchelm seems to have possessed what all messiahs possess: tremendous powers as a preacher and orator. We also have to remember that a large part of his audience would be ignorant peasants who had never heard a really good preacher. As Tanchelm addressed them in the open fields, dressed as a monk, the audiences reacted like modern teenagers to a pop idol. He denounced the Church for its corruption, and told them that if the sacraments were administered by sinful priests they would fail to work. So many were convinced that the churches were soon empty. And when Tanchelm told his followers not to pay taxes to the church (called tithes), they were delighted to follow his advice.

Was Tanchelm a charlatan, or did he really believe he was a messiah? He certainly felt that he had a right to live like a king. He dressed magnificently, and was always surrounded by a large retinue, including twelve men who were supposed to be the twelve disciples. One day he announced that he would become betrothed to the Virgin Mary, and held a ceremony in which he and a sacred statue were joined together in front of a vast crowd who offered their jewelry as an engagement present.

With so many followers, the Church could do nothing about him; he held Utrecht, Antwerp and large areas of the country-side. Finally, in about AD 1115, he was killed by treachery, being stabbed by a priest who had been allowed to approach him. But his influence remained as powerful as ever, and it took another "miracle worker", Norbert of Xanten (who was regarded with favour by the Church) to finally "de-convert" his followers in Antwerp and restore power to the Church.

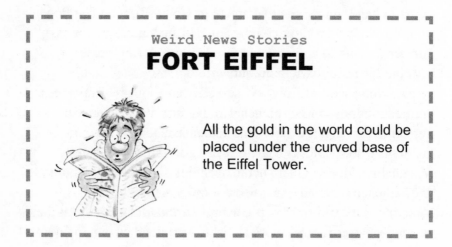

Weird News Stories

FORT EIFFEL

All the gold in the world could be placed under the curved base of the Eiffel Tower.

The Free Spirit Movement – The Wife Who Lost Her Ring
12th century

One popular story of the Middle Ages was about a rich merchant whose wife began to spend a great deal of time in church. When her husband heard rumours that the church consisted of believers in the Free Spirit, he decided to follow her one day. Wearing a disguise, he walked behind her into an underground cavern where – to his surprise – the service began with a dance, in which everyone chose his or her partner. After that, the congregation ate food and drank wine. The husband began to understand why his wife preferred this to the local Catholic church: the service was better.

When the priest stood up, he announced that all human beings are free, and that provided they lived in the spirit of the Lord, they could do what they liked. "We must become one with God." Then he took a young girl and led her to the altar. The two of them removed their clothes. Then the priest turned to the congregation and told them to do the same. "This is the Virgin Mary and I am Jesus. Now do as we do." The girl lay down on the altar, and the priest lay on top of her and, in full view of the congregation, commenced an act of intercourse. Then the congregation each seized his dancing partner, and lay down on the floor.

In the chaos that followed, the wife did not notice as her husband took hold of her hand and pulled off her wedding ring; she was totally absorbed in her partner. Realizing that no one was paying any attention to him, the husband slipped away.

When his wife returned home, he asked her angrily how she dared to give herself to another man, even in the name of religion. She indignantly denied everything, demanding whether, as the wife of a wealthy merchant, he thought she would behave like a prostitute. But when the husband asked her what had happened to her wedding ring, she went pale. Then, as he held it out to her, she realized that he had seen everything, and burst into tears.

The wife was beaten until she bled, but she was more fortunate than the others, who were arrested by inquisitors and burnt at the stake.

The Assassins
In the year 1273, the Venetian traveller Marco Polo passed through the valley of Alamut, in Persia, and saw there the castle of the Old Man of the Mountain, the head of the Persian branch of the sect of Ismailis, or Assassins. By that time, the sect was two hundred years old, and was on the point of being destroyed by the Mongols, who had invaded the Middle East under the leadership of Genghis Khan. According to Marco Polo, the Old Man of the Mountain, whose name was Aloadin, had created a Garden of Paradise in a green valley behind the castle, and filled it with "pavilions and palaces the most elegant that can be imagined", fountains flowing with wine, milk and honey, beautiful *houris* who could sing and dance seductively. The purpose of this Garden was to give his followers a foretaste of Paradise, so that they might be eager to sacrifice their lives for their leader.

When the Old Man wanted an enemy murdered, he would ask for volunteers. These men would be drugged and carried into the secret garden – which, under normal circumstances, was strictly forbidden to all males. They would awake to find themselves apparently in Paradise, with wine, food and damsels at their disposal. After a few days of this, they were again drugged and taken back to the Old Man's fortress. "So when the Old Man would have any prince slain, he would say to such a youth: 'Go thou and slay so-and-so; and when thou returnest, my angels shall bear thee to Paradise.'"

There is evidence that the story may have a foundation in fact.

237

Behind the remains of the castle, which are still visible in the
valley of Alamut, there is a green enclosed valley with a spring.
But it is hardly large enough to have contained "pavilions and
palaces". The Ismailis were a breakaway sect from the orthodox
Moslems; they were the Mohammedan equivalent of Protestants.
After the death of the Prophet Mahomet in 632, his disciple Abu
Bakr was chosen to succeed him, thus becoming the first Caliph
of Islam.

It is a pity that Mahomet, unlike Jesus, never made clear
which of his disciples – or relatives – was to be the rock upon
which his church was to be built. For other Moslems felt that the
Prophet's cousin Ali was a more suitable candidate: the result
was a dissension that split the Moslem world for centuries. The
Sunni – the orthodox Moslems – persecuted and slaughtered
Ali's followers, who were known as the Shi'a. In 680, they
almost succeeded in wiping out their rivals, when seventy of
them – including the Prophet's daughter Fatima – were surprised
and massacred. But the killers overlooked a sick boy – the son
of Fatima; so the rebel tradition lived on.

All this murder and suffering produced powerful religious
emotions among the Shi'a. They set up their own Caliph –
known as the Imam – and they looked forward to the coming of
a messiah (or Mahdi) who would lead them to final victory.
Strange sects proliferated, led by holy men who came out of the
desert. Some believed in reincarnation, others in total moral and
sexual freedom. One sect believed in murder as a religious duty,
strangling their victims with cords; these may be regarded as the
true predecessors of the Assassins.

The Ismailis were a breakaway sect from the original
breakaway sect. When the sixth Imam died, his eldest son Ismail
was passed over for some reason, and his younger brother Musa
appointed. The Ismailis were Moslems who declared that Ismail

was the true Imam: they were also known as Seveners, because they believed that Ismail was the seventh and last Imam. The rest of the Shi'a became known as the Twelvers, for they accepted Musa and his five successors as true Imams. (The line came to an end after the twelfth.)

The Twelvers became the respectable branch of the heretics, differing from orthodox Sunni only on a few points of doctrine. It was the Ismailis who became the true opposition, creating a brilliant and powerful organization with its own philosophy, ritual and literature. They were intellectuals and mystics and fanatics. With such drive and idealism they were bound to come to power eventually.

It was some time around the middle of the eleventh century that the greatest of the Ismaili leaders was born – Hasan bin Sabbah, a man who combined the religious fervour of Saint Augustine with the political astuteness of Lenin. He founded the Order of Assassins, and became the first Old Man of the Mountain. By AD 1300, the Assassins had ceased to exist in the Middle East, at least as a political force.

Weird News Stories

HOTSPOT

Ladak in Kashmir – high in the Himalayas – has the greatest temperature changes in the world. The temperature can drop from 160 degrees in the daytime to 45 degrees at night, and it is possible to experience a drop of 90 degrees by walking from the sunlight into the shade.

The Black Death and the Flagellants

In AD 1345, a horrible disease called the Black Death began to
develop among the corpses of earthquake and flood victims in
China, and was carried by rats along the caravan trails to
Europe. It reached the Crimea, in southern Russia, in 1346. In a
manner that seems sadly typical of human nature, the Tartars
looked around for a scapegoat, and decided that the Christians
must be to blame. They chased the Genoese merchants to their
fortified town of Caffa, then surrounded it and began to
bombard it. But the plague had followed them, and the besiegers
were soon dying in an agony of thirst, with swellings in the
groins and armpits, and the black spots on the skin which gave
the disease its name.

Before they left, the Tartars decided to give the Christians a
taste of the misery they were suffering, and used giant catapults
to lob plague-ridden corpses over the walls. The merchants
carried them immediately to the sea, but they were too late. The
Black Death took a grip in the town, and soon the merchants
decided to flee back to Europe. They took the Black Death with
them. It quickly spread from Messina, the Sicilian port where
the merchants landed, as far as England, killing approximately
half the population.

Again there was a search for scapegoats. In Germany, it was
rumoured that Jews had been poisoning the wells, and fleeing
Jews were seized at Chillon and tortured. Under torture, they
confessed to the charge. They were executed, and there were
massacres of Jews in Provence, at Narbonne and Carcassone,
then all over Germany: Strasbourg, Frankfurt, Mainz, and the
trading towns of the north belonging to the Hanseatic League.
Here Jews were walled in their houses and left to starve; others
were burnt alive.

One of the stranger phenomena that flourished under the

Black Death was the movement known as Flagellants. These had originated about a century earlier in Italy, when various plagues and famines convinced the Italians that God wanted them to show repentance, and took the form of pilgrimages in which people walked naked to the waist, beating themselves with whips or scourges tipped with metal studs. On that occasion it had seemed to work and had been tried periodically since then.

Now the Black Death convinced increasing numbers of people that desperate remedies were necessary.

A letter, supposed to have fallen down from heaven, declaring that only Flagellants would be saved, was first published around 1260, but reappeared in 1343 in the Holy Land – it was supposed to have been delivered by an angel to the Church of St Peter in Jerusalem. Now waves of flagellation swept across Europe with all the hysteria of religious revivals. The Flagellants – mostly fairly respectable "pilgrims" of both sexes – would arrive in a town and hold their ceremony in the main square.

They would strip to the waist, then flog themselves into an increasing state of hysteria until blood ran down to their feet, staining the white linen which was the traditional dress on the lower half of the body. The pilgrimage would last for thirty-three days, and each Flagellant would have taken a vow to flog himself, or herself, three times a day for the whole of that time. A Master also moved among them, thrashing those who had failed in their vows.

As Flagellants themselves carried the plague from city to city, public opinion suddenly turned against them. The magistrates of Erfurt refused them entry, and no one objected. It was best not to wait until the Flagellants were within a town to raise objections, for their own frenzy made them violent, and they were likely to attack the objectors – one Dominican friar in Tournai was stoned to death.

Human beings seem to be glad of an excuse to change their opinions, and only a year after they had been generally regarded with respect and admiration, the Flagellants were suddenly attacked as outcasts and cranks. The Pope issued a bull against them, and the hysteria vanished as abruptly as it had begun.

? ! ? ! ? ! ? ! ? ! ? ! ? ! ?

FASCINATING FACTS

In a Stew
Middle Ages

Apparently, medieval man loved having baths, contrary to popular legend. Many historians believe that people most likely bathed more than they did in the nineteenth century. Ladies often bathed sociably in bathing parties at important castles that had a special room beside the kitchen where hot water could be brought in easily along with perfume, or rose leaves. Lords bathed in their bedchamber in tubs shaped like a half-barrel and containing a stool, so that the occupant could sit and soak long. Cities had public baths, known as "stews" for the populace.

? ! ? ! ? ! ? ! ? ! ? ! ? ! ?

The Bloodfriends

Around 1550, a man named Klaus Ludwig, who lived in Mulhausen in Germany, formed a church in which members were initiated by having sex with a stranger. Like so many messiahs, Ludwig said he was Christ, the son of God, and that these things had been revealed to him. The sacrament was another name for sex. Man was bread and woman was wine, and when they made love, this was Holy Communion. Children born out of such communion were holy. And the members of his congregation could not be killed. His sermons ended with the words "Be fruitful and multiply", and the congregation made haste to undress and do their best to obey.

Ludwig taught that sexual desire is the prompting of the Holy Spirit, so that if a man feels desire for any woman, he should regard it as a message from God. If, of course, the woman happened to be a member of Ludwig's "Chriesterung" (or Bloodfriends), then it was her duty to help him obey the will of the Lord, even if she was another man's wife.

Ludwig told the Bloodfriends to observe great secrecy and to behave like other people. But no doubt some of his congregation was eager to make converts of husbands with attractive wives. Like the congregation in the medieval story, the Bloodfriends were found out and put on trial, although Ludwig himself escaped. One member of the Council of Twelve Judges admitted that he had celebrated Holy Communion with sixteen different women. Three Bloodfriends were executed, and the others were re-converted to a more conventional form of Christianity.

Weird News Stories

BOXING CLEVER

During the whole time he was world champion, boxer Jack Dempsey fought for only 138 minutes. This was because few opponents survived his savage style of fighting for more than a few minutes. On 8 February 1926, he knocked out four men in one round each, and repeated this stunt again four days later.

Sabbatai Zevi circa 1600

One of the most remarkable of all the declared "messiahs" was a Turkish Jew named Sabbatai Zevi (pronounced Shabtight Svy), who at one point seemed about to become one of the most powerful kings in Europe.

Sabbatai was the son of a wealthy merchant of Smyrna (now Izmir) on the coast of Turkey. Born in 1626, he was always of a deeply religious disposition; he spent hours in prayer, and at the age of sixteen, decided to observe a permanent fast, which lasted for six years. He permitted himself to be married to a girl whom his parents chose, but the marriage was never consummated, and she divorced him. The same thing happened to a second wife. He suffered from what would nowadays be called manic-depression, experiencing periods of immense joy and elation, followed by days of suicidal gloom.

In 1648, when Sabbatai was twenty-two a great tragedy

occurred across the sea in Poland. The fierce Cossacks of the
Ukraine rose against the Polish landlords. The Russians and
Poles had traditionally been enemies – in 1618 the Poles had
even tried to put a Pole on the throne of Russia. The Russians
and the Poles both wanted the rich Ukraine. A Cossack leader
called Bogdan Khmelnitsky invaded Poland and challenged the
Polish army. He also set out to destroy the Jews.

A hundred thousand Jews died in this seventeenth-century
holocaust. Thousands of others fled the country, and many went to
Turkey, where there were already wealthy Jewish communities.

When Sabbatai Zevi heard about these massacres he was
appalled. Overwhelmed by a desperate desire to do something
for his people, he suddenly became convinced he was the
Messiah who would lead them back to the Holy Land. And he
began his mission by doing something that horrified his
orthodox fellow Jews – he stood up in the synagogue and
pronounced the name of Jehovah (or Jahweh), that Jews regard
as too sacred to speak. (Instead they used the term Adonai.)

Like all messiahs, he soon collected a small band of followers
who believed every word he said. His fellow orthodox Jews
found this menacing, and banished him when he was twenty-
five. In the Turkish town of Salonika (now Thessaloniki, and a
part of Greece) he gained even more converts. But even his
followers were often puzzled by his strange behaviour. On one
occasion he went around carrying a basket of fish, explaining
that it represented the Age of Pisces, when Jews would be
released from bondage. And on another occasion he shocked the
rabbis by inviting them to a feast, then taking a Scroll of the
Law in his arms as if it were a woman, and carrying it to a
marriage canopy that he had set up; this symbolic marriage of
the Messiah and the Law shocked the orthodox so much that he
was expelled from Salonika.

At the age of thirty-six, surrounded by disciples (who supported him in style) he moved to Jerusalem. There he was seen by a young man who was to become his John the Baptist or St Paul, the son of a Jewish scholar named Nathan Ashkenazi, who was deeply impressed when he saw Sabbatai in the street, but was too young and shy to approach him. It was at this time that Sabbatai found himself a bride, a Polish girl named Sarah, who had escaped the pogrom, become a courtesan (or high-class prostitute), and developed a strange conviction that she was destined to be the bride of the Messiah. The story has it that Sabbatai heard about the beautiful courtesan and sent twelve of his disciples to Leghorn, in Italy, to bring her to him. They were married in March 1664.

In the following year, Sabbatai finally met Nathan, who was now twenty-two (Sabbatai was nearly forty), and allowed himself to be convinced that it was time to announce to the whole world – and not merely to his disciples – that he was the Messiah.

Not all Jews shared this enthusiasm; the orthodox were appalled. "The forbidden" was now allowed, which included incest and promiscuity. The Sabbataians (as they were called) shocked their neighbours by walking around naked at a time when nakedness was regarded as a sin. In the Jewish religion, as in Mohammedanism, women were kept strictly apart. Sabbatai told them they were men's equals and should mix freely with their fellow worshippers. Neither divorce nor infidelity were grounds for a woman to be excluded from full participation in religious rites. Was not the Messiah himself married to a woman who admitted to having been a whore?

Not that Sabbatai's followers were inclined to sexual self-indulgence. They took pride in mortifying the flesh, scourging and starving themselves, rolling naked in the snow, even burying themselves in the earth so only their heads stuck out. It was a frenzy of religious ecstasy, all based on the belief that the Millennium was about to arrive.

Sabbatai decided to go to Constantinople, the Turkish capital, a journey of fourteen days by sea. Once there, he was installed in the castle of Abydos, in Gallipoli, and allowed to continue to live in style, with a succession of distinguished visitors. Unfortunately, one of these was a paranoid old man named Nehemiah ha-Kolen, a Polish scholar who wanted to argue with Sabbatai about the Kabbalah, the Jewish mystical system. He was determined to prove Sabbatai an impostor, or at least, compel him to acknowledge himself, Nehemiah, as an equal. Sabbatai stood up for himself, and probably allowed Nehemiah to see that he regarded him as a bilious and envious old neurotic. Nehemiah hastened away to denounce him to the Sultan as a revolutionary who had admitted that he hoped to usurp the throne. In September 1666, Sabbatai was brought before Sultan Mehmet, and ordered to convert to Islam or die on the spot. Faced with his supreme opportunity for martyrdom, Sabbatai behaved as unpredictably as ever. He promptly removed his Jewish skullcap and accepted a turban instead. He also accepted a new name: Azis Mehmet Effendi. His wife converted too, becoming known as Fatima Radini. The Sultan then granted him a comfortable sinecure as keeper of the palace gates, which carried a generous pension.

Sabbatai, it seemed, had simply abandoned his conviction that he was sent to save the world. He chose comfort – even though he secretly continued to practice Judaism. In public he was a good Mohammedan. But his followers knew better: they realized that this was another of his inexplicable actions.

Unfortunately, he was still subject to these extraordinary swings of mood, in one of which he divorced Sarah – although he took her back again as soon as he was feeling better. He also continued to preach sexual freedom. In due course, these views caused the Sultan embarrassment, and six years after his conversion, Sabbatai was arrested again. This time he was banished to a remote village in Albania, Dulcigno, where he lived on for another four years. Sarah predeceased him in 1674, and he married again. He still had manic moods in which he declared he was the Messiah, but no one paid any attention.

Oddly enough, his "John the Baptist", Nathan Ashkenazi, continued to love and revere him as the Messiah, as did thousands of followers, who regarded his conversion as yet another of his strange god-like actions – rather like those of the Japanese Zen masters who suddenly kick a pupil downstairs. Sabbatai was the only messiah known to history who was able to have it both ways: to proclaim himself a charlatan, and still continue to retain the devotion of his followers. He was the last of the great Jewish messiahs.

Weird News Stories

HARMLESS?

Apparently, cobra venom is quite harmless to drink. But please don't try this at home . . .

The Thugs circa AD 1300–1800

The Thugs (pronounced "tug") came to the attention of Europe after the British annexation of India in the late eighteenth century. At first, the conquerors noted simply that the roads of India seemed to be infested with bands of robbers who strangled their victims. In 1816, a doctor named Robert Sherwood, stationed in Madras, induced some of these robbers to talk to him about their religion. His article "On the Murderers Called Phansigars" appeared in *Asiatic Researches* in 1820, and caused some excitement. Sherwood alleged that the phansigars or Thugs (*phansi* is a noose; *thug* is to cheat) committed murders as a religious duty, and that their aim was the actual killing, rather than the robbery that accompanied it.

The bizarre story caught the imagination of the English, and the word "thug" soon passed into the language. The Thugs, according to Sherwood, lived quietly in their native villages for most of the year, fulfilling their duties as citizens and fathers in a manner that aroused no suspicion. But in the month of pilgrimage (usually November–December) they took to the roads and slaughtered travellers – always taking care to be at least a hundred miles from home.

The method was always the same. The advance guard would locate a band of travellers, then one or two of the Thugs would approach the group and ask if they might travel with it – for protection. A few days later, a few more Thugs would make the same request. This would continue until there were more Thugs than travellers. The killing usually took place in the evening, when the travellers were seated around the fire.

At a given signal, three Thugs would take their place behind each victim. One of them would pass the strangling cloth (or *ruhmal*) around the victim's neck; another would grab his legs and lift them clear of the ground; the third would seize his hands or kneel on his back. Usually, it was all over within seconds. The bodies of the victims were then hacked and mutilated to prevent recognition, and to make them decompose more quickly. The legs were cut off; if there was time, the whole body might be dismembered. Then it was buried.

It was now time for the most important part of the ritual – the ceremony known as *Tuponee*. A tent was usually erected – to shield the Thugs from the sight of travellers. The *kussee*, the consecrated pickaxe (their equivalent of the Christian cross), was placed near the grave: the Thugs sat around in a group. The leader prayed to Kali for wealth and success. A symbolic strangling was enacted, and then all who had taken an active part in the murder ate the "communion sugar" (*goor*), while the chief poured consecrated water on the grave. Once a captured Thug is rumoured to have said: "Let any man once taste of that *goor* and he will be a Thug, though he know all the trades and have all the wealth of the world."

In its earlier days, the members of the sect had been strict in their observance of the rules. It was forbidden to kill women, because Kali was a woman; it was also forbidden to kill religious mendicants, carpenters, metal workers, blind men, pariahs, lepers, mutilated men, and men driving a goat or cow. Greed had caused a gradual relaxation of the rules and it was to this disobedience that the Thugs attributed their decline in fortunes.

In a sense, this was true. Haste and greed meant that bodies were sometimes left unburied, so a search could be instituted more quickly. And in some cases, lack of preparation meant that the killing was bungled. At one the Thugs were pursued back to their own village, and saved from arrest only by the intervention of the villagers (who had been well bribed). Travellers eventually became suspicious of "holy men" or poor Muslims who asked for protection. Better roads (built by the British) meant that Thugs could be pursued more easily. Many of them became informers (or "approvers") to save their own lives. Within a few years, thousands of Thugs had been arrested and brought to trial.

Because he was deeply religious, the Thug was usually scrupulous, honest, kindly, and trustworthy. Many Thugs were rich men who held responsible positions; part of their spoils went to local rajahs or officials, who had no objection to Thugs provided they committed their murders elsewhere. Like the Assassins, most convicted Thugs met their deaths with remarkable bravery, which impressed their British executioners. It is this Jekyll and Hyde character that makes the Thugs so baffling.

One old Thug was the nurse of a family of British children, and obviously regarded his charges with great tenderness. For precisely one month of every year, though, he obtained leave to visit his "sick mother"; when he was arrested as a Thug, the family found it unbelievable, for the Thugs were capable of murdering children as casually as adults.

The male children of Thugs were automatically initiated into the sect. They were first placed in the care of a Thug tutor, who insisted upon absolute obedience, and acted as their religious instructor. (It must be emphasized that the killing was only a part of the ritual of the Thugs, as Communion is of Christians.) At the age of nine or ten, the boys were allowed to act as scouts, and later to watch the killing. At eighteen they were allowed to take part in the killing and eat the *goor*.

By the year 1850, Thuggee had virtually ceased to exist in India. Over 4,000 Thugs had been brought to trial; some were hanged, others sentenced to transportation or life imprisonment.

TO KILL A VAMPIRE

Do vampires still walk in Romania? In 1974 a gypsy woman told of her father's death when she was a girl. According to custom, she said, the body lay in the house awaiting the ceremonial final dressing by the family. After this ceremony it would be carried to the grave uncovered, so that everyone could see that the man was truly dead.

When the family lifted her father's legs to put them in his burial clothes, the limbs were not stiff. Neither were his arms nor the rest of his body. Rigor mortis had not set in. The family stared horrified at him and at each other, and the fearful whispering began.

The story spread among the villagers – people who remembered, or thought they remembered, the vampires that used to roam in the darkness of night. One unmistak-able sign of a vampire is an undecomposed body, kept lifelike by the regular feasting on the blood of the living. Fear licked through the village, and the inhabitants soon came to the house armed with a wooden stake.

The family – bewildered, uncertain, and grief-stricken – fell back. The men tore off the corpse's covering sheet and, in the traditional manner, thrust the stake through the dead man's heart. The vampire – if such it was – was vanquished.

The Mormons 19th Century

Joseph Smith, born in 1805, was the son of a Vermont farmer, and when he was ten, his father, Joseph senior, moved to Palmyra, New York, with his wife and nine children. It was a period of feverish religious activity in America, with various sects – Methodist, Presbyterian, Baptist – expanding at an explosive rate as they made new converts. Joseph's mother Lucy became a convert to Presbyterianism, which had been established by John Calvin in Geneva in 1536, as did two of Joseph's brothers and his sister Sophionia. Joseph attended meetings of the various warring sects, and as he listened to them denouncing one another, he gave a great deal of thought to religion.

In the spring of 1820, after reading a passage in the *Epistle of James* which declared that those in perplexity should ask God, he went into a grove of trees to pray. There he had a revelation – a pillar of light descended, in which he saw two men; one of these pointed to the other and said: "This is my beloved son. Hear him!" Smith then asked God which sect he ought to join, and was told: "None of them." They were all wrong, and all creeds were an abomination in His sight. When Joseph came to his senses he was lying on his back. Back at home he told his mother that he had just learned that Presbyterianism was not true.

Three-and-a-half years later, on 21 September 1823, Joseph was saying his prayers in bed when the light appeared again, and he saw a man dressed in a white robe "whose feet did not touch the floor". The visitor explained that he was an angel called Moroni, who went on to talk at length about the scriptures, then told Joseph that he had written a history of the ancient inhabitants of America on plates of gold. After this, Moroni ascended to heaven in a shaft of light. A few minutes later he reappeared, and repeated everything he had just said, then vanished as before. Soon he was back again, repeating it yet again. The next day, he reappeared as Joseph (in a state of understandable fatigue) was crossing a field, and described where the plates were to be found.

Obeying his instructions, Joseph went to a hill called Cumorah, about four miles away. On the top, he found a large stone which he levered up with a pole. In the hole underneath was a box, and in this he found some gold plates, a breastplate, and a pair of silver spectacles – which Moroni had called Urim and Thummim – and which would enable him to translate the words on the gold plates. Smith was not allowed to take them yet. The angel showed him a vision of the heavens, and also of the Prince of Darkness and his legions, then explained that Joseph must spend four years of preparation in order to become worthy of translating the plates.

In 1827, Smith was finally allowed to take the gold plates away with him. He carried them home in a borrowed buggy, but seems to have showed them to no one, not even his wife Emma, who went with him to collect them. Two months later, with fifty dollars presented by his first disciple, a farmer called Martin Harris, Smith and his wife went to Harmony, Pennsylvania, and there Joseph settled down to translating the plates with the aid of the silver spectacles.

He did this behind a screen, so that no one actuallly saw the plates. Martin Harris called at some point, and took away a piece of paper with a transcription of some of the characters on it. They were apparently in a script called "reformed Egyptian" and Harris showed them to a New York professor named Anton, who gave him a certificate saying that the characters were genuine. But when he heard that they had been obtained from an angel Anton tore up his certificate.

So *The Book of Mormon* came into existence. It told how
America had been originally settled by people from the Tower
of Babel in the fifth century AD. These settlers gradually
degenerated into men of violence. Eleven hundred years later,
more settlers arrived in Chile, including four brothers. From one
of the brothers, who was fair, descended a white race, the
Nephites; from the other three, who were dark, descended the
Indians (or Lamanites). After his death on the cross, Jesus Christ
appeared in America and preached the gospel. And in AD 385,
after the Nephites were almost wiped out by the Lamanites near
the Hill Cumorah, their prophet Mormon wrote the history,
which was then buried in the hill.

Martin Harris mortgaged his farm to provide the cash for
publication, and *The Book of Mormon* appeared in 1830.
Meanwhile, the gold plates had been returned to the angel
Moroni, no one but Smith having even glimpsed them, although
a young schoolteacher named Oliver Cowdery helped with the
translation from the other side of the screen. The first 116 pages
of the manuscript had already been lost when Martin Harris's
indignant wife threw them on the fire.

The Latter-Day Saints – as the Mormons now called
themselves – decided to move west. The "missionaries" had
already established a church in Kirtland, Ohio. Problems arose.
The citizens of Kirtland objected to the Saints as the citizens of
Munster had objected to the Anabaptists. In 1836, the Saints
established their own bank and printed their own money; in
1837, it collapsed, causing much hardship; five of Smith's
twelve "apostles" denounced him as a fallen prophet, and left.
Smith saw it all as a test of the faithful.

Other Saints had already established themselves in Missouri;
Smith joined them there. By now even Martin Harris and Oliver
Cowdery had left in disillusionment. When angry mobs drove

the Mormons out of Missouri – after Smith had spent several months in jail – they moved on to found the town of Nauvoo in Illinois. But Illinois's inhabitants proved to be as hostile as those of Missouri. Smith may have made things worse in July 1843 by publishing a document declaring that God had ordained polygamy, or "plural marriage" – although at this stage it was not openly announced. (Smith himself must have been practising plural marriage long before he announced its legality, for he seems to have married at least twenty-seven women, and possibly as many as forty-eight.) Finally, a dispute with the governor became so bitter that, early in 1844, Smith decided it was time to go further west to found a City of the Saints.

Governor Ford was worried as the surrounding communities armed themselves and talked about massacring the Saints. In June, Smith and his associates – including his brother Hyrum – were charged with "riot". Convinced that he would be killed, he decided to flee, but then changed his mind and returned to give himself up. This seemed to defuse the threatened violence, and Joseph Smith, his brother Hyrum, and two followers were lodged in Carthage jail.

On 27 June 1844, at four in the afternoon, a hundred men rushed the jail. Governor Ford had marched his forces off to Nauvoo to restore order, and there were only eight men in charge of the prisoners. Hyrum was shot by a bullet that came through the window, and collapsed on the floor. Joseph Smith opened the door and emptied his six-shooter into the mob. Then the attackers flung open the door and began shooting.

One of the disciples, John Taylor, tried to jump out of the window, but was hit by a bullet. Joseph Smith attempted to leave the same way, and was hit several times; he fell out of the window, twenty feet from the ground. Staring out of the window after him, the other disciple, Willard Richards, saw that he seemed to be dead.

It was left to Smith's chief lieutenant, Brigham Young, to lead the Saints on their great trek westward, to the place where, in 1847, they founded Salt Lake City. With tremendous energy they irrigated the desert, and arranged the transportation of thousands of converts from Europe. (The Mormons always attached great importance to proselytizing.) When Young announced the doctrine of polygamy in 1852, he was deprived of the governorship of the territory. "Plural marriage" was finally disowned by the Church in 1890, but when Young died in 1877 he had seventeen wives and fifty-six children.

Mormonism – as can be seen – always aroused fierce opposition. Smith's advocacy of plural marriage was undoubtedly one of the chief causes of later hostility to the Mormons. In the mid-1920s, Brigham H. Roberts, the official historian of the Mormon Church, appealed to Church leaders to "help him resolve problems" about *The Book of Mormon,* one of which was that it contained so many similarities to a book called *A View of the Hebrews* published in 1823 by the Reverend Ethan Smith.

Another problem was that *The Book of Mormon* refers to the ancient Hebrews' use of steel, and to domestic animals that were unknown in ancient times. Referring to many similar discrepancies, Roberts concluded: "The evidence, I sorrowfully submit, points to Joseph Smith as their creator." Whether or not this is true, Smith remains one of the most charismatic and influential messiahs of the nineteenth century.

257

The Cargo Cult

The inhabitants of the Melanesian islands in the Pacific have, since their first contact with Western travellers, developed the so-called "cargo cults". Cargo refers in the islanders' pidgin to goods of any kind given by visitors.

First contact occurred with the arrival of the Russian Count Nikolai Mikiouho-Maclay in 1871. He was received as a god, due to the incredible nature of his transport, a Russian frigate, and his gifts, which were amazing to a culture that was still effectively in the Stone Age. German traders and Christian missionaries only served to reinforce the natives' awe and faith. The basic tenets of the religion became set: visitors who give "cargo" are good, those who do not are evil, as they withhold what are seen as spiritual gifts.

In 1940 the Americans built a military base on the Melanesian island of Tanna in the southern Hebrides. Cargo planes zoomed in and out leaving radios, canned beer and other Western necessities. The natives observed the American service men in uniform; and wishing to bring more planes and enjoy similar luxuries they improvised uniforms and spoke into empty beer cans, as they had seen the Americans speak into microphones.

What began as adoration and emulation soon turned to dissatisfaction as their rituals failed to get the desired response. The faith changed its nature, becoming a conviction that the Western presence on the island was of the wrong kind. Soon a messiah would come to give the natives what the Americans refused to give them. John Frum or Jonfrum was the name that the natives gave this messiah, although the reason is not clear. Some say that Frum is a corruption of broom, to sweep away the white man. Others put forward the simpler explanation that the name is derived from "John from America". He is described as a small man with bleached hair, a high-pitched voice and a coat with shiny buttons.

The cult persists in many different forms on each of the remote Melanesian islands. What began as simple worship of Westerners has developed into an entire liberation theology in a very short time: John Frum will one day arrive and hand over all of the "cargo" to the natives, while getting rid of the Westerners. After that the islanders would live on as normal, only richer and happier than before.

WEIRD TALES

The Mystery of the *Mary Celeste*

On a calm afternoon of 5 December 1872 the English ship *Dei Gratia* sighted a two-masted brig pursuing an erratic course in the North Atlantic, midway between the Azores and the coast of Portugal. As they came closer they could see that she was sailing with only her jib and foretop mast staysail set; moreover, the jib was set to port, while the vessel was on a starboard tack – a sure sign to any sailor that the ship was out of control. The *Mary Celeste* had set sail for Genoa with a cargo of crude alcohol on 5 November, ten days before the *Dei Gratia* had sailed for Gibraltar; yet now, a month later, she was drifting in mid-Atlantic with no sign of life. Morehouse sent three men to investigate, led by his first mate Oliver Deveau, a man of great physical strength and courage. As they clambered aboard they saw that the ship's decks were deserted; a search below revealed that there was not a living soul on board. But the lifeboat was missing, indicating that Captain Briggs had decided to abandon ship. There was a great deal of water below decks; two sails had been blown away, and the lower foretop sails were hanging by their corners. Yet the ship seemed seaworthy, and was certainly in no danger of sinking. Both forward and aft storage lockers contained a plentiful supply of food and water.

The seamen's chests were still in the crew's quarters, an indication of the haste in which the ship had been deserted. But a search of the captain's cabin revealed that the navigation instruments and navigation log were missing. The last entry in the general log was dated 25 November; it meant that the Mary Celeste had sailed without crew for at least nine days, and that she was now some 700 miles north-east of her last recorded position.

Apart from Captain Briggs and a crew of seven, the *Mary Celeste* had also sailed with Briggs's wife Sarah and his two-year-old daughter Sophia Matilda. It was suggested that two of the *Dei Gratia*'s crew should sail the *Mary Celeste* to Gibraltar, for this they would receive £5,000 salvage money.

Both ships arrived in Gibraltar harbour six days later. And instead of the welcome he expected, Deveau was greeted by an English bureaucrat who nailed an order of immediate arrest to the *Mary Celeste*'s mainmast. The date significantly was Friday the thirteenth.

British officials at Gibraltar seemed to suspect either mutiny or some Yankee plot – the latter theory based on the fact that Captain Morehouse and Captain Briggs had been friends, and had apparently dined together the day before the *Mary Celeste* had sailed from New York. But at the inquiry that followed, the idea of mutiny seemed to have gained favour. To back this theory, the Court of Inquiry was shown an axe-mark on one of the ship's rails. In addition to this the ship had scoring on her hull that was described as a crude attempt to make the ship look as if she had hit rocks, and a stained sword that was found beneath the captain's bunk. All this, it was claimed, pointed to the crew getting drunk, killing the master and his family, and escaping in the ship's boat. The Americans were insulted by what they felt was a slur on the honour of the US Merchant Navy, and denied this story. They pointed out that Briggs was not only known to be a fair man who was not likely to provoke his crew to mutiny, but also that he ran a dry ship; the only alcohol on the Mary Celeste was the cargo. Even a thirsty sailor would not be likely to drink more than a mouthful of crude alcohol – it would cause severe stomach pains and eventual blindness. Besides, if the crew had mutinied, why should they leave behind their sea-chests together with such items as family photographs, razors, and sea-boots?

The British Admiralty remained unconvinced, but had to admit that if the alternative theory was correct, and Briggs and Morehouse had decided to make a false claim for salvage,

Briggs would actually have lost by the deal. He was part-owner of the ship, and his share of any salvage would have come to a fraction of what he could have made by selling his share in the normal way.

In March 1873 the court was finally forced to admit that it was unable to decide why the *Mary Celeste* had been abandoned, the first time in its history that it had failed to come to a definite conclusion. The *Dei Gratia*'s owners were awarded one-fifth of the value of the *Mary Celeste* and her cargo. The brig herself was returned to her owner, who lost no time in selling her the moment she got back to New York.

So, what happened? Once we know that the life-boat was missing, we at least know one thing for certain: that the crew abandoned ship, apparently in great haste – the wheel was not lashed, an indication that the ship was abandoned in a hurry. The question then presents itself: what could have caused everyone on board to abandon the ship in such a hurry?

Only one explanation covers all the facts. Briggs had never shipped crude alcohol before, and being a typical New England puritan, undoubtedly mistrusted it. The change in temperature between New York and the Azores would have caused casks of alcohol to sweat and leak. The night of storms, in which the barrels would have been shaken violently, would have caused vapour to form inside the casks, slowly building up pressure until the lids of two or three blew off.

The explosion, though basically harmless, might have blown the hatches off the cargo hold on to the deck in the positions in which Deveau later found them. Convinced that the whole ship was about to explode, Briggs ordered everyone into the lifeboat. In his haste, he failed to take the one simple precaution that would have saved their lives – to secure the lifeboat to the *Mary Celeste* by a few hundred yards of cable. The sea was fairly calm when the boat was lowered, as we know from the last entry in the log, but the evidence of the torn sails indicates that the ship then encountered severe gales. We may conjecture that the rising wind blew the *Mary Celeste* into the distance; while the crew in the lifeboat rowed frantically in a futile effort to catch up. The remainder of the story is tragically obvious.

HERE'S THE BELL, HERE'S THE STEEPLE . . .

In November 2003, a Romanian priest is said to have appealed to his young parishioners to abstain from having sex in his church's steeple. "There are used condoms everywhere," he supposedly complained. "I even found some hanging on the bell's chain." Local police chief Lucian Sfetcu, however, said little could be done to resolve the problem: "We give out hundreds of fines for this activity."

Chapter Sixteen

A Brief, Unreliable History of . . .

Hollywood and the Movies

Hollywood and The Movies

Everything you ever wanted to know about the silver screen.

1

As early as the 1860s devices to show moving images were being created. Zoetropes and praxinoscopes showed a series of images at high enough speed to fool the eye into seeing continuous motion. But the first surviving film is *Roundhay Garden Scene* by Louis Le Prince.

2

Early in the twentieth century, cinema flourished in both America and Europe. But the war in Europe meant that it was Hollywood that became the world centre of film-making in the 1920s. Early films were silent, accompanied by a pianist or group of musicians, and covered a wide variety of subjects and styles including fantasy as in Georges Méliès *Le Voyage dans la Lune*, which featured a rather bizarre depiction of the man in the moon.

3

As great wealth came to Hollywood, scandal inevitably followed. News stories such as the Fatty Arbuckle manslaughter trial gave Hollywood the reputation of being Sin City, and film directors' propensity for using naked flesh and sexual suggestion led to the moral crackdown of the Hays Code. This created the bizarre situation that a man and woman could only be depicted in bed if they were dressed with one foot on the floor.

4

Clara Bow was the first "It Girl" following her successful run in movies in the mid-1920s. She had a tormented and difficult life in spite of her stardom. Rumours spread of her complicated private life and sexual escapades. Perhaps her own quote sums it up the best: "The more I see of men, the more I like dogs."

5

In 1927 *The Jazz Singer* became the first successful sound film. Over the next few years Hollywood underwent a transformation as actors and actresses whose voices didn't work on screen were replaced by a new generation of stars.

6

Through the Great Depression, movies provided a powerful means of mental escape from the difficulties of everyday life. Stars of the thirties such as Clark Gable and Greta Garbo and great directors such as John Ford defined the classic Hollywood period.

7

In the late 1940s, Hollywood faced two huge challenges – the rise of television, the bug-eyed monster which rivalled its power, and the antitrust laws that threatened to bring down the studio system. In spite of this great films continued to be made throughout the 1950s and 1960s. Indeed it can be argued that film's status as a great art was enhanced by the need to surpass the offerings of television.

8

The early success of "New Hollywood" films such as *Bonnie and Clyde* and *Easy Rider* helped open the door to the big budget film-makers of the 1970s, in particular directors such as Spielberg, Ford, Coppola, and Martin Scorsese.

9

Three films defined the 1970s: *The Godfather*, *Jaws* and *Star Wars*. Great achievement though each was in its way, the effect of the latter two films was probably negative in the long run. Hollywood became focused on the blockbuster movie, to the detriment of intelligent, small-budget film-making.

10

In spite of the overbearing influence of the blockbuster, directors as diverse as Spike Lee, Steven Soderbergh, Kevin Smith, and Quentin Tarantino continued to keep Hollywood challenging through the 1980s and 1990s, so that even today, in the age of video and illegal movie downloads, Hollywood remains the centre of the film-making world.

Future Bingo

The future history of the world is hard to predict. But as we look forward in fear and hope, why not have some fun while we're waiting?

Keep this **Future Bingo** sheet to hand, and cross off any events that actually happen in the future. If you get a full page of amazing future events, then shout out "House".

If you send the finished page to the **Future Bingo** corporation (at an address yet to be determined), you may even receive a mystery prize . . .

Johnny Rotten statue unveiled in House of Commons.	Smoking banned in Kalahari Desert.
Peruvian Empire colonizes Australia.	Ming the Merciless attacks Kremlin.
Terrorists admit they were getting things a bit out of proportion.	Pope implicated in bellhop crack scandal.

Chapter Seventeen

Weird News: Plot Against the King

273

One afternoon King James VI of Scotland, who lived between 1566 and 1625 – later to become King James I of England – was out hunting near Perth, when his friend Alexander Ruthven, a beautiful boy and the brother of the much loved Earl of Gowrie, rode up to him and asked him over for supper in Gowrie's castle nearby. After some hemming and hawing, the King, who liked the company of beautiful boys, agreed and Alexander rode off home to make preparations.

The King duly arrived at Gowrie's castle with a small company of men and was given a modest supper – due to the lack of time for preparation. According to some reports the Earl of Gowrie behaved rather strangely at supper and didn't spend as much time talking to the King as he ought to have. The King, at least, was keen to tell everyone that the Earl had behaved strangely. Just as the meal was ending, young Alexander and the King went off together to an upper room in the castle where – according to the King – Ruthven promised to introduce the King to a Jesuit spy he had caught that afternoon.

About half an hour into the enquiry, which, for reasons best known to the King, involved him and Ruthven being locked by themselves in a room containing nothing but a bed, a number of people in the street below the bedroom window heard a loud hullabaloo emanating from the chamber in which they knew the King was conducting a special, private investigation.

Worried for their monarch's safety, they quickly alerted the King's soldiers who rushed up to the room and found James and Alexander on their own, apparently wrestling. Alexander was immediately killed by the guards. The Earl of Gowrie ran to the bedroom to discover his brother dead on the floor. King James immediately claimed that the two men had plotted to kill him and that he had somehow miraculously escaped the effects of

274

treason – well, what else could he say? – and Gowrie too was instantaneously executed.

A huge number of influential people all over Europe didn't believe the King, who immediately started ferreting around for evidence to incriminate the Earl and his brother. Not a single person could be found to give evidence against the young nobles, and there was a storm of protest. According to the brutal custom of the time, the corpses of the brothers were taken to Edinburgh and subjected to the pantomime of a trial. In October (when the brothers had already been dead for ten weeks in mid-summer) the rotting bodies were hanged, drawn, and quartered and their heads were stuck on poles above Cowgate in Edinburgh. None of this prevented James succeeding to the English throne just three years later.

Weird News Stories

HOLY HOSE

In 1998, Church elders and several firefighters baptized 2000 people in Charlotte, North Carolina – by fire hose. "It's not the water," C. B. Gibson of the United House of Prayer for All People supposedly explained, "it's the belief you have in it."

WEIRD TALES

The Disappearance of Agatha Christie

In 1926 Agatha Christie was involved in a mystery that sounds like the plot of one of her own novels. But unlike the fictional crimes unravelled by Hercule Poirot, this puzzle has never been satisfactorily solved. On the freezing cold night of 3 December 1926 she left her home at Sunningdale, in Berkshire, and disappeared.

At eleven the next morning, a Superintendent in the Surrey Police was handed a report on a "road accident" at Newlands Corner, just outside Guildford. Agatha Christie's Morris two-seater had been found halfway down a grassy bank with its bonnet buried in a clump of bushes. There was no sign of the driver, but she had clearly not intended to go far, because she had left her fur coat in the car.

An extensive search of the area around Newlands Corner was organized and deep-sea divers investigated the Silent Pool, an allegedly bottomless lake in the vicinity. In the *Daily Mail* the following Sunday there was an interview with her husband in which he admitted "that my wife had discussed the possibility of disappearing at will. Some time ago she told her sister, 'I could disappear if I wished and set about it carefully . . .'"

On 14 December, eleven days after her disappearance, the head waiter in the Hydropathic Hotel in Harrogate, North Yorkshire, looked more closely at a female guest and recognized her from newspaper photographs as the missing novelist. He rang the Yorkshire police, who contacted her home. She had been staying in the hotel for a week and a half. She had taken a good room on the first floor at seven guineas a week, and had apparently seemed "normal and happy", and "sang, danced, played billiards, read the newspaper reports of the disappearance, chatted with her fellow guests, and went for walks".

When her husband went to collect her. "She only seemed to regard him as an acquaintance whose identity she could not quite fix," said the hotel's manager. Archibald Christie told the press: "She has suffered from the most complete loss of memory and I do not think she knows who she is." A doctor later confirmed that she was suffering from loss of memory. But Lord Ritchie-Calder later remembered how little she seemed to correspond with the usual condition of amnesia. When she vanished, she had been wearing a green knitted skirt, a grey cardigan and a velour hat, and carried a few pounds in her purse. When she was found she was stylishly dressed, and had three hundred pounds on her. She had told other guests in the hotel that she was a visitor from South Africa.

Agatha Christie divorced her husband (who wed Miss Neele) and in 1930 married Professor Sir Max Mallowan. But for the rest of her life she refused to discuss her disappearance, and would only grant interviews on condition that it was not mentioned. Her biographer, Janet Morgan, accepts that it was a case of nervous breakdown, followed by amnesia. Yet questions remain unanswered. Where did she obtain the clothes and the money to go to Harrogate? Why did she register under the surname of her husband's mistress? And is it possible to believe that her amnesia was so complete that, while behaving perfectly normally, she was able to read accounts of her own disappearance, look at photographs of herself, and still not even suspect her identity?

CHRIST'S MASS AT CHRISTMAS

Did you know that our word Christmas is derived from the Middle English usage "Christ's Mass." In Medieval England there were, in fact, three Masses celebrated on Christmas Day. The first and most characteristic was at midnight (the Angel's Mass), catching up the notion that the light of salvation appeared at the darkest moment of the darkest date in the very depth of winter. The second Christmas Mass came at dawn (the Shepherd's Mass), and the third during the day (the Mass of the Divine Word). The season of Advent, the forty days of leading up to Christmas, has been observed in the Western Church since the year AD 500. St Nicholas was a very popular medieval saint, and his feast day came in Advent (6 December), but he did not play his part in Christmas as Santa Claus until after the Reformation.

Chapter Eighteen

A Brief, Unreliable History of . . .

The 20th Century

The 20th Century

Everything you ever wanted to know about
the century of chaos, warfare, dictators, sex,
drugs and rock and roll.

1

The start of the twentieth century was a very different time to today. No television, no computers, no Hollywood, no Celebrity Wrestling Idol, no Paris Hilton. In short there wasn't much to do, and nothing much to talk about. But there were several large European Empires, wondering what to do with their huge pile of guns, bombs, and soldiers.

2

Unsurprisingly, war broke out in 1914. Most people thought that the war would be jolly good fun, a bit like a scout outing to an outdoor playground, and that it would be over by Christmas, with a glorious victory for whichever empire they happened to be living in.

3

Instead, the war went on for four long years, became the most savage war in history to date, and only ended after several million young men had died. The gold standard had collapsed, never to be successfully restored, and the Russian Revolution had led to the victory of communism, which would soon become Stalinism, the first of a series of mad dictators who helped define the century. All in all, the war hadn't been such a good idea after all.

4

In spite of all this, the 1920s turned out to be one big party. Much champagne was drunk by wealthy financiers and flappers, the stock market soared and everybody was going to be rich forever. Until 1929 when the stock market crashed and everybody lost all their money.

5

The Great Depression had a variety of consequences. The American Midwest was depopulated as the dustbowl years and big business farming combined to drive people away. Franklin Roosevelt introduced the New Deal, completely transforming the role of American government (for better or worse depending on your political hue). Meanwhile in Europe, the Germans became increasingly ticked off as their currency collapsed and the years of post-War poverty extended. As a result Adolf Hitler started to gain popularity. You all know what happens next.

6

The Second World War was like a big budget remake of a blockbuster movie. Worse than the First on every level. More countries, more deaths, more civilians killed, more genocides, more countries' economies ruined, and more atomic bombs. The only good thing was that most sensible people came out of it thinking that a Third World War might not be such a good idea.

7

The 1950s were defined by cold war paranoia, rock and roll and increasing prosperity. America and Russia skirmished around the world in a variety of revolutions and uprisings without ever coming directly into conflict.

8

The 1960s: the Vietnam War, the Summer of Love, the Beatles, hippies, Carnaby Street, self-indulgent twaddle from men in beards, kaftans, tie-dye. You know all about it because you saw it in a movie once.

9

The 1970s – the world economy teeeters on the brink of collapse. Strikes, shortages, inflation, war, famine, this must be nearly the end of the world, right?

10

Wrong! The 1980s! Shoulder pads! Dallas! New Romantics!
The fall of the Berlin Wall! The 1990s, housing crashes, rave
culture, the rebirth of Eastern Europe, Kurt Cobain. By the end
of the decade everything was on such an even keel that Francis
Fukuyama declared the "end of history", meaning that
everything in the world would just go on being much the same
forever and ever.

11

He was wrong . . .

Future Bingo

The future history of the world is hard to predict. But as we look forward in fear and hope, why not have some fun while we're waiting?

Keep this **Future Bingo** sheet to hand, and cross off any events that actually happen in the future. If you get a full page of amazing future events, then shout out "House".

If you send the finished page to the **Future Bingo** corporation (at an address yet to be determined), you may even receive a mystery prize . . .

Teenagers collectively apologise to parents for "being a pain in the butt".	Save the Cockroach campaign fears roach extinction is imminent.
Rhinoceroses attack Buckingham Palace.	Ballet banned in Nevada.
Socks with sandals become fashionable.	Internet completely replaces human conversation.

Chapter Nineteen

More Religious Mania

John III Sobieski 1624–1696, **King of Poland** 1674–96
In 1683, John Sobieski's military skills drove the invading
Turks back from the walls of Vienna, altering forever the history
of central Europe. He soon announced victory to the Pope. "I
came, I saw . . ." he declared. And? "God conquered." [A play
on Julius Caesar's famous remark: "Veni, vidi, vici." ("I came, I
saw, I conquered.")

John Bunyan, English preacher and writer 1628–1688
The author of *The Pilgrim's Progress*, John Bunyan, had little
worldly success. He became a lay preacher in the army at
sixteen and his friend was killed standing next to him. At
seventeen, his mother died. At twenty-one he was a husband,
and at twenty-seven he became a widower, the father of four
young children, one of them blind. At thirty-two, he was jailed
for preaching without a government licence and his second wife
suddenly went into labour and delivered a child who died soon
after. He was offered his freedom if he would stop preaching the
gospel, but is famously said to have replied, "If I am freed
today, I will preach tomorrow." Bunyan spent the next twelve
years of his life in prison. In spite of his difficult life, he
faithfully wrote and preached of God's grace and goodness.

? ! ? ! ? ! ? ! ? ! ? ! ? ! ?

FASCINATING FACTS

English Rose
16th Century

The most famous warship during the reign of
the Tudors was the *Mary Rose*, built in 1510. In
1545, the *Mary Rose* flipped onto her side off
the coast of Portsmouth. All the sailors fell into
the sea and 750 of them drowned. The ship was
salvaged in 1982, nearly 400 years later. She is
now on display in Portsmouth, England.

? ! ? ! ? ! ? ! ? ! ? ! ? ! ?

William Warburton 1698–1779
William Warburton was the Bishop of Gloucester between 1759
and 1779 and a literary scholar. In the eighteenth century, during
a debate in the House of Lords on the Test Laws, which obliged
candidates for public office to profess allegiance to the Anglican
faith, the Earl of Sandwich is said to have remarked, "I have
heard frequent use of the words 'orthodoxy' and 'heterodoxy'
but I confess myself at a loss to know precisely what they
mean." Bishop Warburton explained: "Orthodoxy is my doxy,"
he whispered. "Heterodoxy is another man's doxy."

Grisly Tales from History
Old Bones
Dynasties of Ancient China

Fortune telling has always been popular with the Chinese. During the days of the Shang Dynasty (1122 BC–256 BC) they did this by cracking the bone from a dead animal and reading the fracture lines (like reading tea leaves). They were known as oracle bones. When they were found many years later people then thought they were "magic" dragon bones and crushed them to use in medicinal potions.

Philip Dormer Stanhope, Fourth Earl of Chesterfield
1694–1773

Philip Stanhope, Lord Chesterfield, was an English politician, diplomat, and writer. His sister, secretly entertaining hopes that he would be converted to Methodism, tried to persuade her ill brother to visit a Methodist seminary in Wales to recuperate. Apparently, as she extolled the virtues of the setting's spectacular mountain views, Chesterfield, suspecting what she was up to, interrupted her: "I do not love mountains," he is said to have announced. "When your ladyship's faith has removed them, I will go thither with all my heart."

John Owen 17th Century

As the great American Puritan leader John Owen lay on his deathbed, his secretary wrote a letter on his behalf to a friend containing the words, "I am still in the land of the living." Owen then ordered his secretary to stop. He requested that she change that to, "I am yet in the land of the dying, but I hope soon to be in the land of the living."

Philip Dormer Stanhope, Fourth Earl of Chesterfield
1694–1773

The eighteenth-century English preacher George Whitefield was so popular that the Privy Council one day discussed how to control his vast evangelical rallies. "Make him a bishop," Lord Chesterfield is said to have suggested, "and you will silence him at once."

Robert Boyle 1627–1691

The great Irish-born English physicist and chemist Robert Boyle is noted for his pioneering experiments with gases and chemical elements, culminating in his formulation of Boyle's Law in 1662. He was also a surprisingly devout man. After being frightened by a thunderstorm in Geneva as a boy, he turned to God and wrote essays on religion, later learning Hebrew and Aramaic, and financing missionary work in the Orient. He also left a bequest for the establishment of the Boyle Lectures for the defence of Christianity against unbelievers. Nonetheless, in 1680, he was elected president of the eminent Royal Society. He apparently declined to accept because he disapproved of the form of the oath.

293

? ! ? ! ? ! ? ! ? ! ? ! ? ! ?

Liz and John
16th Century

Elizabeth I is credited with being responsible for the world's first flushing toilet. She was so offended by the palace toilets that she had a flushing one invented for her by Sir John Harington. This could be why it's still sometimes referred to as "the John" to this day.

? ! ? ! ? ! ? ! ? ! ? ! ? ! ?

Jacques Benigne Bossuet 1627–1704

Jacques Bossuet was a French Roman Catholic bishop and preacher. Shortly after Louis XIV named Jacques Bossuet Bishop of Meaux in 1681, the king solicited some of the town's citizens for their opinions of the new bishop. They liked him fairly well, they replied. "Fairly well? Why, what's wrong with him?" Louis asked. "Well, to tell Your Majesty the truth, we should have preferred a bishop who had completed his education," the villagers explained. "Whenever we call to see him we are told that he is at his studies."

Grisly Tales from History
Writers' Block
Dynasties of Ancient China

The first Emperor of China was called Qin Shi Huangdi (260 BC–210 BC). He took the throne at the age of nine and was by all accounts a terrible tyrant. He had all the books and papers of the past destroyed because he wanted things done his way. He also buried alive all the writers to make sure they didn't write any more!

George Frideric Handel 1685–1759
Not long after the London debut of Handel's *Messiah* in 1743, the composer was apparently complimented by Lord Kinnoul on his "noble entertainment." "My Lord, I should be sorry if I only entertained them," Handel replied. "I wished to make them *better*."

John Wesley 1703–1791
It is said that while preaching a sermon one day, John Wesley, the English evangelist noted for his role in the foundation of Methodism, was dismayed to find that quite a few members of his congregation were asleep. Apparently he cried "Fire! Fire!" to get the guilty parishioners to wake up. "Where?" they asked,

looking around. "In hell," Wesley is said to have replied, "for those who sleep under the preaching of the Word!" During his lifetime, John Wesley preached a remarkable 40,000 sermons.

Samuel Johnson 1709–1784
Samuel Johnson was an English journalist, critic, poet and famous lexicographer. His biographer, James Boswell, attended a Quaker meeting one Sunday morning, where he heard a woman preaching for the first time. Apparently he later related the remarkable experience to Dr Johnson. "Sir," Johnson is said to have remarked, "a woman's preaching is like a dog's walking on his hind legs. It is not done well, but you are surprised to find it done at all."

John Wesley 1703–1791
Wesley was an English religious leader whose message of repentance and faith was apparently so appealing that one hoodlum, sent by Anglican leaders to disrupt a Wesleyan meeting, found himself unable to carry out his intention. As he raised his hand to strike a blow to Wesley's head, he brought it down with surprising delicacy, simply declaring, "What soft hair he has!"

Christoph Willibald Gluck, German composer 1714–1787
Towards the end of his life, the German composer Christoph Gluck was asked whether a bass or a tenor should sing the part of Christ in *The Last Judgment*. "If you wait a little," Gluck famously replied, "I shall be able to tell you from personal experience."

Grisly Tales from History
Dead Man's Chest
Ancient Egypt

Julius Caesar was imprisoned by
pirates who took him hostage,
demanding a large amount of
money. The ransom was paid for his release and he
subsequently hunted down the pirates who did it and had
all of them killed.

John Montagu, Fourth Earl of Sandwich 1718–1792
John Montague, Lord Sandwich, was a British politician, the
First Lord of the Admiralty between 1748 and 1751, and
between 1771 and 1782. He is said to have brought in a large
baboon while hosting a formal dinner one evening. The baboon
was apparently dressed in clerical garb and was supposedly
there to say grace. His chaplain, grievously offended,
immediately rose to leave the room. "I did not know," he
declared, turning in the doorway, "that your lordship had so near
a relative in holy orders."

FASCINATING FACTS

A Traveller's Tale
18th Century

In the late eighteenth century a traveller's tale passed around London. It told of two Welsh missionaries who, having been captured by American Indians and sentenced to death, began lamenting to each other in Welsh. The tribe of Indians were astounded: they, too, spoke Welsh. The missionaries were freed and received the Indians' heartfelt apologies.

The great Welsh Druid Edward Williams, or Iolo Morganwg, took the story so seriously that he raised backing for an expedition to investigate the Welsh Indians. The theory put forward for their existence traced their roots to the expedition of the Prince Madoc, who had set sail westwards in the twelfth century and had never been heard of again. Williams was eventually prevented from going on the expedition by failing health, but one of his followers, John Evans, did attempt the journey. He eventually died in New Orleans after many adventures, having been unable to locate the Welsh Indians.

John Wilkes 1725–1797

John Wilkes was an American politician and journalist, and a
member of the English Parliament between 1757 and 1764,
noted for his libel arrest in 1763, his exile to Paris between 1764
and 1768, and his political comeback as a Middlesex MP from
1774. A staunch Roman Catholic once confronted the Protestant
John Wilkes and asked him. "Where was your religion before
Luther?" Wilkes is said to have retorted "Did you wash your
face this morning?" When the Catholic admitted that he had.
Wilkes told him "Then, pray where was your face before it was
washed?"

Thomas Paine, British political theorist and writer
1737–1809

In 1802 Thomas Paine escaped the guillotine, by chance – he
had been elected to the French Convention and subsequently
imprisoned by Robespierre – and emigrated to the United States.
One day while travelling through Baltimore, he was approached
by a Swedenborgian minister who had recognized him as the
author of *The Age of Reason* whose deistic thesis the minister
was clearly eager to discuss.

"I am minister of the New Jerusalem Church here," he
declared, "and we explain the true meaning of the Scripture. The
key had been lost above four thousand years, but we have found
it . . ."

"It must," Paine replied testily, "have been very rusty."

Ethan Allen 1738–1889

Ethan Allen was an American patriot, the leader of the "Green
Mountain Boys" during the Revolutionary War. A stern
Calvinist minister delivered a sermon one Sunday attended by
Ethan Allen and several of his colleagues. "Many shall strive to

enter, but shall not be able," the minister cried. "Indeed, God's grace was sufficient," he continued, "to include one in ten, but not one in twenty would endeavour to avail himself of the offered salvation . . . Moreover, not one in fifty was the true object of God's solicitude, and not one in eighty was fit . . ." At this point, Allen is said to have collected his hat and left the pew. "I'm off, boys," he announced. "Any one of you can take my chance!"

Rowland Hill 1744–1833
According to folklore a number of people sought shelter in a chapel during a heavy downpour. The British preacher Rowland Hill happened to be preaching there at the time.

"People who make religion their cloak are rightly censured," he apparently declared, "but I consider that those who make it their umbrella are not much better."

Richard Porson 1759–1808
Richard Porson was a British classical scholar noted for his editions of the plays of Euripides – and also for his love of liquor. He and a Trinitarian friend were discussing the nature of the Trinity when a carriage containing three men passed by. "There," the friend is said to have exclaimed, "that's an illustration of the Trinity." Porson, however, disagreed and told his friend, "You must show me one man in three buggies – if you can!"

Grisly Tales from History
Cut Up in Greece
Ancient Greece

The Ptolemaic period was a time of the emergence of new thoughts and ideas in the arts and sciences in the two major civilizations, the Egyptian and the Greek. Ptolemy the Third let a physician called Erasistratus practice his surgery skills on criminals who had been given the death sentence. No anaesthetic was used! The fourth Ptolemy killed his father because he couldn't wait to become King and the most famous Queen of Egypt, Cleopatra, killed her brother so that she could take the throne. After she married Roman Mark Anthony in 31 BC she lost a war with the Roman army and Egypt subsequently became a Roman state. Cleopatra was so upset she killed herself with a bite from an asp.

John Dalton 1766–1844

John Dalton was a British chemist noted for his study of colour-blindness, for his pioneering work on the properties of gases, and for his consequent formulation of atomic theory. In 1832, he received a doctorate from Oxford University and was duly presented to King William IV. Though tradition demanded that he wear a scarlet robe, Dalton happened to be a Quaker. Dalton's solution, when the robe was brought before him, was to declare that the garment was completely gray and therefore wearable.

Apparently, Dalton also happened to be completely colourblind.

William Lamb Melbourne, Second Viscount 1779–1848

William Melbourne was an English statesman, the Secretary for
Ireland from 1826 to 1827, Home Secretary from 1830 to 1834,
and Prime Minister in 1834, and again from 1835 to 1841. He
once had to sit through a long evangelical sermon on the
consequences of sin. Not noted for his appreciation of religious
experience, Melbourne apparently replied that he had always
been a supporter of the church, and always upheld the clergy,
but pointed out that it was really too bad to have to listen to a
sermon like the one that morning. He is said to have later
complained about the preacher having actually insisted upon
"applying religion to a man's personal life."

Jean Henri Merle d'Aubigne, Swiss Protestant divine
1794–1872

During a stay with the Scottish preacher Thomas Chalmers and
his family, the Swiss Protestant Jean d'Aubigne was given a
kippered herring for breakfast. He is said to have asked about
the meaning of the word "kippered" and was told that it meant
"kept" or "preserved". Apparently as he later led the household
in their morning prayers, he asked the Good Lord to see that
they be "kept, preserved – and kippered."

? ! ? ! ? ! ? ! ? ! ? ! ? ! ?

FASCINATING FACTS

Victoria and Bertie
19th Century

It is said that initially Queen Victoria wasn't too keen on marrying her cousin Albert at first but she asked him to marry her anyway. (No man can propose to a queen!) He said yes, apparently because he had been told to. However, when Prince Albert died of typhoid in 1861, Queen Victoria was reportedly so upset that she was not seen in public afterwards for ten years. Even after that she wore black until she died to show she was still in mourning.

? ! ? ! ? ! ? ! ? ! ? ! ? ! ?

Lionel Nathan Rothschild 1808–1879

Lionel Nathan Rothschild, of the prominent family of European bankers, became the first Jewish member of the British House of Commons in 1847. However, because he found the standard oath of office unacceptable to his Jewish faith Rothschild refused to assume his seat until it was changed. Parliament eventually agreed and Rothschild dutifully took his seat . . . eleven years later!

Abraham Lincoln 1809–1865

Abraham Lincoln, popularly known as "Honest Abe" represented the State of Illinois in Congress between 1847 and 1860, and served as the sixteenth president of the United States of America between 1861 and 1865. He is noted for his anti-slavery election ticket, which precipitated the secession of the Southern states and his leadership of the Union forces during the ensuing Civil War. He also made the Emancipation Proclamation of 1863 which freed Southern slaves and drafted the Thirteenth Amendment which prohibited slavery in the USA in 1865.

Abraham Lincoln ran for Congress as a Whig in 1846 against an evangelical Methodist named Peter Cartwright. Apparently, one day during the campaign, he attended a religious meeting at which Cartwright, after a stirring welcome, invited everyone who hoped to go to heaven to rise. Several of the congregation did so. "Now," Cartwright supposedly said, "those who do not wish to go to hell will stand!" With these words, everyone else stood up, with a single notable exception, Lincoln himself.

Cartwright asked Mr Lincoln, "Where you are going?" Lincoln stood and replied. "I came here as a respectful listener. I did not know I was to be singled out by Brother Cartwright. I believe in treating religious matters with due solemnity. I admit that the questions propounded by Brother Cartwright are of great importance. I did not feel called upon to answer as the rest did. Brother Cartwright asks me directly where I am going. I desire to reply with equal directness: I am going to Congress!"

Grisly Tales from History
The Minoan Goddess
Ancient Greece

The Minoans were the first civilization
of ancient Greece and they lived on
the island of Crete from around
2100 BC to 1500 BC. They were apparently a rich and
peaceful people. However, they were taken over by the
Mycenaeans around 1500 BC. The Mycenaeans
worshipped Goddesses instead of Gods and would deal
with famine or earthquake disasters by attacking
neighbouring countries to steal what they needed.

William Ewart Gladstone 1809–1898
William Gladstone, who was the Liberal prime minister of Great
Britain on four separate occasions, apparently once said, "One
thing I have against the clergy both of the country and in the
towns: I think they are not severe enough on congregations.
They do not sufficiently lay upon the souls and consciences of
their hearers their moral obligations, and probe their hearts and
bring up their whole lives and actions to the bar of conscience."

Henry Ward Beecher 1813–1887
Henry Ward Beecher was an American Congregational minister
and author, the brother of Harriet Beecher Stowe. He is noted
for his fervent campaigns for the abolition of slavery. During a
visit to Henry Ward Beecher one day, Robert Ingersoll noticed a
beautiful globe depicting the various constellations and stars of

the heavens. Ingersoll asked Beecher who had made it. "Who made it?" Beecher replied, seizing the opportunity to attack his guest's well-known agnosticism. "Why, nobody made it. It just happened."

? ! ? ! ? ! ? ! ? ! ? ! ? ! ?

FASCINATING FACTS

Hitler's Real Name
20th Century

Did you know that Adolf Hitler's father was originally called Adolf Schicklgrüber but he changed his name to Hitler before Adolf was born? One wonders if Hitler would have been quite such a prominent historical figure, had he been known by his father's original name. It's difficult to be a feared dictator when your name makes people giggle.

? ! ? ! ? ! ? ! ? ! ? ! ? ! ?

Louis Antoine Jullien 1812–1910
Louis Jullien was a French composer and conductor, noted for his London promenade concerts. Not long after he was born, at Sisteron in the Basses Alpes, his father, a violinist, was invited to play a concerto with the local Philharmonic Society orchestra.

Jullien's father graciously decided to invite one of the musicians to be the child's godfather.

A problem arose, however, when each of the orchestra's thirty-six members vied for the privilege. An agreement was finally reached whereby the infant – held by the society's secretary at the font – was duly baptized with all thirty-six names. Jullien's full name, while cumbersome, proved a useful source of pseudonyms for his musical compositions.

Henry Ward Beecher 1813–1887
Henry Ward Beecher rejected harsh Calvinism and so concocted an interesting romantic idea of religion as a warm, indiscriminate bath of love. To be truly religious, he said, you must sin, since Christ can't very well save you if you don't.

Elizabeth Cady Stanton 1815–1902
A married clergyman is said to have once reproached the famous feminist and social reformer Elizabeth Cady Stanton as she spoke in public at a women's rights convention in Rochester, New York. "The apostle Paul enjoined silence upon women," he apparently told her. "Why don't you mind him?" "The apostle Paul also enjoined celibacy upon the clergy," Stanton replied. "Why don't you mind him?"

Grisly Tales from History
Sacrificial Beasts
Roman Empire

The Romans had different gods for different things and tried to keep all the gods happy all of the time lest things go badly for them. Many animals were killed on temple altars as sacrifices to the gods, especially cockerels and rams that were considered holy creatures and therefore killed most often. When cows and other large animals were sacrificed they would be killed and their insides would be taken out for the priest to examine the liver. If it wasn't deemed to be healthy or was in some way badly formed it was considered a bad omen. In these cases, they sometimes found a human to sacrifice as well.

Daniel Abramovich Chwolson 1819–1911

Daniel Chwolson was a Russian archaeologist, who was appointed Professor of Oriental Languages at the University of St Petersburg in 1855, and Professor of Hebrew at the St Petersburg Academy in 1858.

He was apparently once asked whether his decision to join the Orthodox Church had been made out of conviction or expediency. "I accepted baptism entirely out of conviction," Chwolson is said to have replied, "the conviction that it is better to be a Professor in the Academy in St Petersburg than a teacher in a school in Vilna."

Edward Everett Hale 1822–1909

During his time as chaplain of the US Senate, writer Edward
Hale, the nephew of Nathan Hale was once asked, "Dr Hale, do
you pray for the Senate?" "No," he allegedly replied. "I look at
the Senators and pray for the people."

Matthew Arnold 1822–1888

The English poet and critic, Matthew Arnold, who was
Professor of Poetry at Oxford between 1857 and 1867, was
apparently famed for his staunch reserve and critical eye. There
was much comment after his death in 1888. Robert Louis
Stevenson is reputed to have said, "Poor Matt. He's gone to
Heaven, no doubt, but he won't like God."

Thomas Huxley 1825–1895

Known as "Darwin's Bulldog", Thomas Huxley was a British
biologist, philosopher, and paleontologist, noted for his eloquent
defence of Charles Darwin's evolutionary theories, and for his
coinage of the term "agnostic".

In Oxford in June 1860 there was an historic meeting
between the supporters of Charles Darwin's theory of evolution
by natural selection and the Church. In opposing corners were
Samuel Wilberforce, the Bishop of Oxford, and Thomas
Huxley, who spoke for the Darwinian camp. Wilberforce
unexpectedly delivered a savage speech against Darwin and
Huxley: "If anyone were to be willing to trace his descent
through an ape as his grandfather," he demanded of Huxley,
"would he be willing to trace his descent similarly on the side of
his grand*mother*?" "A man has no reason to be ashamed of
having an ape for his grandfather," Huxley is famously said to
have declared. "If there were an ancestor whom I should feel
shame in recalling, it would rather be a man who, not content

with an equivocal success in his own sphere of activity, plunges into scientific questions with which he has no real acquaintance!"

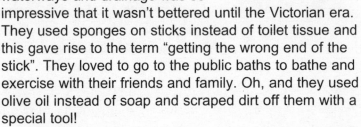

Grisly Tales from History
Roman Plumbing
Roman Empire

The Romans gave us the beginning of plumbing. Their system of waterways and drainage was so impressive that it wasn't bettered until the Victorian era. They used sponges on sticks instead of toilet tissue and this gave rise to the term "getting the wrong end of the stick". They loved to go to the public baths to bathe and exercise with their friends and family. Oh, and they used olive oil instead of soap and scraped dirt off them with a special tool!

Thomas Jonathan "Stonewall" Jackson 1824–1863
The American Confederate general "Stonewall" Jackson once blamed the date, a Sunday, for a failed attempt to destroy the canal leading to Washington. In order to avoid breaking the Sabbath again, Jackson planned to attack on a Monday – using gunpowder obtained on the previous Saturday. The quartermaster, however, unable to find powder at such short notice, was obliged to procure it on the Sunday. When Jackson

learned of this unfortunate fact, he promptly sent for "Monday powder." "I desire," he told his colonel, "that you will see that the powder that is used for this expedition is not the powder that was procured on Sunday."

WEIRD TALES

The Loch Ness Monster

Loch Ness, the largest of Britain's lakes, is twenty-two miles long and about a mile wide; at its greatest depth, it is 950 feet deep. The loch is part of the Great Glen, which runs like a deep crack right across Scotland, from one coast to the other; it opened up between 300 and 400 million years ago as a result of earthquakes, and was then deepened by glaciers. At the southern end of the loch is the small town of Fort Augustus; and, at its northern end, Inverness.

The first account of the Loch Ness monster to appear in print was in AD 565, in *The Life of St Columba*. This tells (in Volume 6, Book 11, Chapter 27) how the saint arrived at a ferry on the banks of the loch and found some men preparing to bury a comrade who had been bitten to death by a water monster while he was swimming. The saint ordered one of his own followers to swim across the loch. The monster heard the splashing and swam towards him, at which the saint made the sign of the cross and commanded the creature to go away; the terrified monster obeyed.

Other reportings down the centuries are more difficult to pin down; in his book on the monster, Nicholas Witchell mentions a number of references to the "beast" or "water kelpie" (fairy) of Loch Ness in old books between 1600 and 1800. And after Commander Rupert Gould published a book on the monster in 1934, a Dr D. Mackenzie of Balnain wrote to Gould claiming to have seen it in 1871 or 1872, looking rather like an upturned boat but moving at great speed, "wriggling and churning up the water". Alex Campbell, the water bailiff, reported that a crofter named Alexander MacDonald had seen the monster in 1802 and reported it to one of Campbell's ancestors.

Until the eighteenth century, the loch had been practically inaccessible, except by winding trackways; it was not until 1731 that General Wade began work on the road that runs from Fort Augustus up the south side of the loch (although Fort Augustus was not so christened until 1742). But this steep road, which makes a long detour inland, was obviously not the shortest distance between Fort Augustus and Inverness; the most direct route would run along the northern shore. In the early 1930s a road was finally hacked and blasted out of this northern shore, and vast quantities of rock were dumped down the steep sides of Loch Ness. The road had only just been completed in April 1933, and it was on 14 April that Mr and Mrs John Mackay, proprietors of the Drumnadrochit Hotel, were returning home from a trip to Inverness.

It was about three in the afternoon when Mrs Mackay pointed and said, "What's that, John?" The water in the middle of the loch was in a state of commotion; at first she thought it was two ducks fighting, then realized that the area of disturbance was too wide. As her husband pulled up they saw some large animal in the middle of the surging water; then as they watched, the creature swam towards Aldourie pier on the other side of the loch. For a moment they glimpsed two black humps, which rose and fell in an undulating manner; then the creature made a half-turn and sank from sight.

The Mackays made no attempt to publicize their story, but gossip about the sighting reached a young water bailiff, Alex Campbell, who also happened to be local correspondent for the *Inverness Courier.* He called on the Mackays, and his report went into the Courier on 2 May, more than two weeks after the sighting occurred. The editor is said to have remarked: "If it's as big as they say, it's not a creature it's a monster." And so the "Loch Ness Monster" acquired its name.

The first "modern" report of the monster had occurred in 1930. The *Northern Chronicle* reported that three young men who were out in a boat fishing on 22 July of that year, and saw a loud commotion in the water about 600 yards away, with some large creature swimming towards them just below the surface. They said that it turned away when it was about 300 yards away. The young men commented that it was "certainly not a basking shark or a seal". That summer of 1933 was one of the hottest on record, and by the end of the summer the Loch Ness Monster was known to readers all over the British Isles; it was still to become a worldwide sensation.

By now the monster had also been sighted on land. On a peaceful summer afternoon, 22 July 1933, Mr and Mrs George Spicer were on their way back to London after a holiday in the Highlands.

At about four o'clock they were driving along the southern road from Inverness to Fort William (the original General Wade road) and were on the mid-portion between Dores and Foyers. About two hundred yards ahead of them they saw a trunk-like object apparently stretching across the road. Then they saw that it was in motion, and that they were looking at a long neck. This was soon followed by a grey body, about five feet high (Mr Spicer said later, "It was horrible – an abomination.") which moved across the road in jerks. Because they were on a slope, they could not see whether it had legs or not, and by the time their car had reached the top of the slope it had vanished into the undergrowth opposite. It seemed to be carrying something on its back.

They saw no tail, and the drawing that Commander Gould made later under their direction justifies Mr Spicer's description of a "huge snail with a long neck". Commander Rupert Gould, who had published a book on the monster in 1934, heard of this sighting and thought it was a hoax. However, after he had interviewed the Spicers in London, he had no doubt that they were telling the truth. The Spicers still seemed shaken and upset. It was later suggested the object over the monster's shoulder could have been a dead sheep.

In November 1933 "Nessie" was photographed for the first time. Hugh Gray, an employee of the British Aluminium Company, was walking on a wooded bluff, fifty feet above the

314

loch, near Foyers. He had seen the monster on a previous occasion, and was now carrying a camera. It was Sunday 12 November 1933, a sunny morning, and Gray sat down for a moment to look out over the loch. As he did so he saw the monster rising up out of the water, about two hundred yards away. He raised his camera and snapped it while it was two or three feet above the surface of the water.

It is not the clearest of all photographs – it is easy to focus attention on the dark shadow and to overlook the vague, greyish bulk of the creature rising from the water above it. This was only one of five shots; the others seem to have been even less satisfactory. Gray was so ambivalent about the sighting – afraid of being subjected to derision – that he left the film in his camera for two weeks, when his brother took it to be developed. It appeared in the Scottish *Daily Record* and the London *Daily Sketch* on 6 December 1933, together with a statement from the Kodak film company that the negative had not been retouched. But Professor Graham Kerr, a zoologist at Glasgow University, declared that he found it utterly unconvincing as a photograph of any living thing. It was the beginning of the "debunking" of the monster, in which major zoologists were to be prominent for many decades to come.

After the initial excitement, most people were willing to accept the view of sceptics that the monster had been a cynical invention of people involved in the Highland tourist business; if so, it had certainly succeeded, for Loch Ness hotels were crowded throughout the summer. One of the most interesting sightings of 1934 went virtually unnoticed. On 26 May Brother Richard Horan, of St Benedict's Abbey, was working in the abbey boathouse when he heard a noise in the water, and saw the monster looking at him from a distance of about thirty yards. It had a graceful neck with a broad white stripe down its front, and a muzzle like a seal's. Three other people corroborated his sighting. In the December of the following year, a Miss Rena Mackenzie also saw the monster fairly close, and noted that its head seemed tiny, and that the underside of its throat was white.

A man named John Maclean, who saw the monster in July 1938, saw the head and neck only twenty yards away, and said that it was obviously in the act of swallowing food, opening and closing its mouth, and tossing back its head "in exactly the same manner that a cormorant does after it has swallowed a fish". When the creature dived Maclean and his wife saw two humps. They described it as being about eighteen feet long, and said that at close quarters its skin was dark brown and "like that of a horse when wet and glistening".

Each of these sightings enables us to form a clearer picture of the monster. And in July 1958 the water bailiff Alex Campbell had a sighting which confirmed something he had believed for many years – that there must be more than one creature; he saw one lying quietly near St Benedict's Abbey while another (visible as a large black hump) headed across the loch, churning the surface of the water. (Many accounts indicate that the animals can move at high speed.)

In June 1965, Frank Searle was parked in a lay-by near Invermoriston and chatting to some hitchhikers when he saw a dark object break the surface, and realized he had at last seen the monster. His excitement was so great that in 1969 he gave up his job and pitched his tent by Loch Ness, where he was to remain for the next four years. In August 1971 he saw the tail at close quarters as the monster dived; his impression was of an alligator's tail, "seven feet long, dark and nobbly on top, smooth dirty white underneath". In November 1971 he got his first photograph of the monster – a dark hump in a swirl of water; he admitted that it was "inconclusive". In the following five years he obtained at least ten of the best pictures of the monster taken so far, including one showing the swan-like neck rising out of the water, and another showing both the neck and one of the humps. These were published in his *Nessie: Seven Years in Search of the Monster* in 1976.

In 1972, a team of investigators led by Dr Robert H. Rines took some remarkable underwater photographs. One of these showed very clearly an object like a large flipper, perhaps eight feet long. A 1975 photograph showed a long-necked creature and its front flipper; this was particularly impressive because the sonar evidence – waves of sound reflected back from the creature – made it clear that this was not some freak of the light or a piece of floating wreckage.

Yet in spite of this, monster-hunters in the 1970s and 1980s began to experience an increasing sense of frustration. Most people still regard the question of the monster's existence as an open one, and the majority of scientists still regard the whole thing as something of a joke.

Grisly Tales from History
We Who Are About To Die
Roman Empire

The Romans loved their blood sports. They watched gladiators fight in special arenas called amphitheatres. Gladiators always began their routine by calling "We who are about to die salute you" to the Emperor. Most gladiators were slaves or criminals forced to take up the role. If they were really good they could earn their freedom.

Chapter Twenty

A Brief, Unreliable History of . . .
The First Millennium AD

The First Millennium AD

Everything you ever wanted to know about
the millennium that came second in the
Best Millennium Ever awards at last
year's Golden Globes.

First Century

The big events of the first century AD were the life of Jesus and
the spread of the Roman Empire. But there were other
highlights. Lions became extinct in Western Europe, the Goths
moved to Poland, Vesuvius erupted, burying Pompeii, the
Romans started to persecute Christians, and Buddhism spread to
China.

Second Century

The Roman Empire reached its greatest extent under the Five
Good Emperors, Hadrian built a big wall to keep the Scots in
Scotland, while the Han Dynasty ruled China. Ptolemy compiled
a map of all the visible stars. The Roman Empire started to
decline after the mad Emperor Commodus declared himself to
be the reincarnation of Hercules.

Third Century

The Roman Empire started to dissolve into anarchy and civil war, Christianity continued to spread, the first pair of glasses were made for a short-sighted Syrian princess. And most importantly of all, the crop of maize made its way from Mexico into North America, allowing the development of popcorn by Native Americans.

Fourth Century

Constantine became the last Emperor to rule both the Eastern and Western part of the Empire, and moved his capital to Constantinople (now Istanbul). St Augustine of Hippo lived and wrote his theological masterworks. And the *Kama Sutra* was written, leading to many centuries of cricked necks and dislocated backs as lovers attempted to emulate its more ridiculous positions.

Fifth Century

The Roman Empire ended, although the Byzantine Empire survived. The relationship between man and horse became more complex as the stirrup was invented in China and metal horseshoes became common in Western Europe. After the sack of Rome, Europe started to fall back in to barbarism, and Attila the Hun was given the Man of the Century award.

Sixth Century

The Franks (cheese-eating surrender monkeys) became the
dominant force in Europe, the monastery on Iona was founded
by St Columba (a major moment in the spread of Christianity),
there were riots and black death in Constantinople. And King
Arthur supposedly fought his last at the Battle of Camlann.

Seventh Century

Islam was started by the Prophet Muhammad. The Bulgars
arrived in the Balkans to start the Bulgarian Empire. The relic of
the True Cross was stolen from Jerusalem. The Chinese
introduced their first paper currency.

Eighth Century

In North Africa and Spain, Islamic Arabs spread. Late in the
century the Vikings from Scandinavia started to rape and pillage
across Northern Europe. Most people in Europe at this stage
were living in mud huts in daily fear for their lives from pirates,
invaders, or their weird neighbours. The Renaissance seemed an
awfully long way off.

Ninth Century

This was deep into the bad times. The Holy Roman Empire had
a limited range due to the chaos of central Europe. Major events
included the life of Alfred the Great in the UK, the writing of

the epic Beowulf, and the start of the decay of Latin into various romantic languages across Europe. The first Norse settlers arrived in Iceland and wondered why they'd bothered. There may also have been a female pope, Joan, although this could be a rumour that was started later on.

Tenth Century

A tumultuous century, this was the nadir of the Dark Ages in Europe, with bloody battles and confusion reigning across the continent. It was a time of political upheaval in China, and the point at which the Islamic caliphate was at its greatest extent. The first Mayan Kingdom declined, but the Toltecs rose in Mexico. A thousand years after the birth of Christ, fears of the end of the world grew in Christian lands as the millennium approached.

Future Bingo

The future history of the world is hard to predict. But as we look forward in fear and hope, why not have some fun while we're waiting?

Keep this **Future Bingo** sheet to hand, and cross off any events that actually happen in the future. If you get a full page of amazing future events, then shout out "House".

If you send the finished page to the **Future Bingo** corporation (at an address yet to be determined), you may even receive a mystery prize . . .

David Beckham becomes patron saint of Argentina.	Last ice in Antarctica melts.
President gives varmints protected species status.	Hollywood recognizes own worthlessness, cancels Oscars, vows to do better next year.
Hell freezes over.	Moonshine found to cure cancer.

Chapter Twenty-one

Weird News: Silly Cycles

In 1897 Thomas Bennet of 69 High Holborn announced a splendid new design of bicycle. The front wheel and handlebars looked pretty much the same as they do on a modern bike. The pedals, however, were mounted on a single huge cog communicating directly with a tiny cog at the centre of the back wheel.

The back wheel was very unusual. It was heavy and spoked and had sixteen free-spinning tiny wheels mounted around the edge. The crucial element of Adam's design was that the driver should sit directly on top of this curious wheel. As the pedals went round forwards, the central back wheel would rotate backwards and the tiny wheels around the edge would sort of squidge the cycle forwards. As Adams explained it:

"The weight of the rider is perpendicular to the centre of the small wheel which is under him. Immediately the toothed wheel is turned ever so little by the larger toothed wheel from the crank, the weight of the rider is lifted off the centre of the small wheel under him. This, coupled with the power put forth by the rider on to the pedal, causes the smaller wheel under him to, as it were, slip from under him with tremendous velocity (the heavier the rider the greater the velocity) on to the next small wheel."

The principle of the thing, thought Adams, "was the same as that by which a roller-skater fell over: when the hind wheels of the skate slip forward from under him, his weight goes off the centre and he loses his equilibrium and goes on to the back of his head with great force (the heavier the man, the heavier he falls). If the skater could have only kept his equilibrium," explains Adams, "he would have gone forward as fast as his skate travelled, instead of being left behind on the floor." By this process, the mad inventor thought that his bicycle could travel at sixty miles per hour.

The number of mistakes involved in this design is frighteningly high. Adams ignores every law of motion in constructing his potty bike. As the modern scientist Alan Sutton points out in his book *A Victorian World of Science* (Iowa, 1986), any rider pedalling Adams's bike would remain stock still. The ludicrous back wheel would simply whizz round, with all the little wheels spinning in the opposite direction as they hit the ground or the rider's bottom.

Future Bingo

The future history of the world is hard to predict. But as we look forward in fear and hope, why not have some fun while we're waiting?

Keep this **Future Bingo** sheet to hand, and cross off any events that actually happen in the future. If you get a full page of amazing future events, then shout out "House".

If you send the finished page to the **Future Bingo** corporation (at an address yet to be determined), you may even receive a mystery prize . . .

American South secedes from North.	Seagulls divebomb Chinese premier at UN shindig.
White House painted pink.	Tomorrow cancelled due to lack of interest.
Venusian terraforming completed.	Philip K. Dick awarded posthumous Nobel Prize, accepts from alternative universe.

Chapter Twenty-two

More Scandalous Royal Tales

Bonnie Prince Charlie 1720–1788

Charles Edward Stuart, then known as the Young Pretender or
Bonnie Prince Charlie, was born in Rome in 1720. He was the
grandson of the deposed King James II of England (also of
Scotland) and the son of the "Old Pretender", James Stuart, who
had twice tried unsuccessfully to invade Scotland in order to
seize the British throne. In 1745 the Young Pretender made his
own attempt to put his father on the throne. He landed in
Scotland with a handful of men, raised an army, and invaded
England, but the lack of promised support from England and
France forced him to retreat to Scotland, where his forces
suffered a devastating defeat at the Battle of Culloden Moor in
April, 1746. Thereafter Bonnie Prince Charlie became a fugitive.

After several months on the run, he met Flora MacDonald on
the Scottish island of Benbecula. Her foster father, Clanranald,
commanded the government troops on Benbecula, and her
fiancé, Allan MacDonald, was a military officer. The islanders
feared official reprisals if the fugitive was discovered on
Benbecula, so Flora agreed to help Charles escape.After hiding
him for a week Flora disguised Charles as her maid, "Betty
Burke", and smuggled him to the island of Skye. Guards there
did apparently comment on Betty's odd appearance but let them
go anyway. Flora turned Charles over to his sympathizers in
Skye, who helped him make his way safely to France. He and
Flora never met again, although legend has it that Flora kept a
lock of his hair to remember him by. However, it seems that
Bonnie Prince Charlie's luck had run out and he became
something of an alcoholic drifter. Eventually he settled in Rome
as the "Duke of Albany" and married a princess, but they
separated after less than ten years of marriage. Charles died in
1788.

Flora was arrested and imprisoned in the Tower of London

334

for her role in the Young Pretender's escape. After her release she became something of a celebrity. Flora died in 1790 and was buried on the island of Skye, wrapped (so the story goes) in Bonnie Prince Charlie's bedsheet.

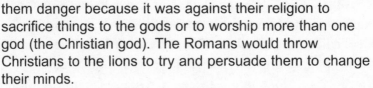

Grisly Tales from History

Unlucky
Christians

Roman Empire

Whenever the Romans encountered a Christian they thought the Christians would bring them danger because it was against their religion to sacrifice things to the gods or to worship more than one god (the Christian god). The Romans would throw Christians to the lions to try and persuade them to change their minds.

Queen Boadicea AD 26

Boadicea (also spelled Boudicca or Boudica) was born into a royal family around AD 26. She married Prasutagus, king of the Iceni a tribe located in what is now Norfolk, England. Prasutagus ruled under the auspices of the Romans, who had probably put him on the throne in return for his assistance when they invaded England in AD 43.

Upon Prasutagus's death around the year AD 59, the kingdom passed into the hands of the Romans. The king had hoped the Romans would allow his two teenage daughters to keep half of his property, but instead the Romans took over completely.

When Boadicea complained, she was publicly flogged and forced to watch as her daughters were raped.

Furious, Queen Boadicea, described by one Roman historian as a tall, terrifying-looking woman with fierce eyes, a harsh voice, and very long red hair, became the leader of a violent uprising against Roman rule. The rebels destroyed London, Colchester, and other cities, slaughtering some 70,000 people.

But the Romans quickly put down the rebellion by defeating the undisciplined Britons in a ferocious battle (the exact site of which is uncertain). According to one account, Boadicea then killed herself with poison so she would not fall into Roman hands. Boadicea's name means "victorious", as does Victoria, and in Victorian times she came to be viewed as a heroic symbol of Britain.

King George IV, the drunken bridegroom 18th Century
The future King George IV married a German princess named Caroline Amelia of Brunswick–Wolfenbuttel on 8 April 1795. According to rumour, the prince was so drunk that he had to be held up by his groomsmen and, in the words of one eye-witness, he "looked like death". He continued to drink after the ceremony and, unsurprisingly, ended up spending his wedding night passed out on the bedroom floor.

Although the Prince of Wales and his new bride were first cousins, they had met just three days before they became man and wife. The prince, who was known for his loose morals and lavish spending, agreed to the marriage at the urging of his current mistress, Lady Jersey, and his father, King George III, who had promised to pay off his debts. The king, of course, just wanted his son to settle down. And what was Lady Jersey's motive? According to one account, she hoped that his new wife would make him forget his old wife.

? ! ? ! ? ! ? ! ? ! ? ! ? ! ?

Training the Spies
20th Century

During the Second World War, training for spies and special agents was done at secret London addresses and large country houses. The agents were taught things like how to get in and out of places without anyone finding out, picking locks, and breaking safes. They had mock interrogations where they had to pretend that they had been captured by the enemy so that they could learn how to avoid giving away any information. They were also taught how to dress in disguise and were given clothing right down to the last detail. Special clothes were made in workshops for whatever "character" the agents had to become to ensure that the style of clothing was exactly right. They were given new weapons such as silent pistols and guns that looked like pens. Female spies might have hidden cameras in their handbags. One way of sending a secret message was to write on the agent's body in invisible ink that could only be seen by putting a special chemical onto the skin. They had forged papers and left secret messages in walls.

? ! ? ! ? ! ? ! ? ! ? ! ? ! ?

**Princess Caroline Amelia of Brunswick Wolfenbuttel, a
scandalous princess** 18th Century

King George IV and Caroline were mismatched from the start. By
all accounts, he was an immaculate dandy; she rarely bathed,
prided herself on dressing quickly, and, in the words of one historian, "smelt like a farmyard". He was interested in art and architecture; she, according to the prince's friend Lord Malmesbury, had
"a light and flighty mind and was flippant and sarcastic." George
and Caroline spent their honeymoon in a rented house filled with
George's disreputable friends, who, according to Caroline, "were
constantly drunk and filthy, sleeping and snoring in bouts on the
sofas." George had also brought along his mistress, Lady Jersey.
No wonder Caroline said the place "resembled a bad brothel much
more than a palace."

Somehow the bride and groom managed to put aside their
differences long enough to consummate the marriage and their
daughter Charlotte was born in 1796. Women had no right to
custody of their children under the laws of the time, and when
Caroline left George in December 1797 she was forced to leave
her daughter behind as well. Caroline consoled herself by living
lavishly and supposedly having affairs with anyone who took
her fancy, male or female. By 1805 Caroline's reputation was so
bad that the government launched a "Delicate Investigation" into
her private life. She had adopted a little boy, and gossip had it
that he was actually her own illegitimate son.

In 1814, Caroline decided to leave England but sad news
reached Caroline in 1818. Her daughter had died. Now George
had no heir, and Caroline feared he would have her killed so he
could remarry. Now King George IV, he was determined to
prevent Caroline from being crowned queen. Caroline was
equally determined that she would be crowned. It was the
beginning of a royal battle.

Caroline returned to England in 1820 to fight for her right to be queen. The ordinary people of Britain were vehemently on her side. Mobs roamed the streets shouting "Long live the queen!" and attacking those who refused to join in. Even the Duke of Wellington, a national hero, was accosted by a group of Caroline supporters. He apparently told them, "Well, gentlemen, since you will have it so, God save the queen and may all your wives be like her."

So great was the outcry against the king that a revolution was feared. George remained obstinate, and his ministers had no choice but to introduce a bill into the House of Lords preventing her from becoming queen and dissolving their marriage. The debate over this bill lasted more than three months and much of the focus was on Caroline's relationship with an Italian manservant who while travelling with her had allegedly shared her tent and her bathtub.

Public opinion remained with Caroline even though in the end the "Bill of Pains and Penalties" was defeated by a vote of 123 to 95. The king would not get his divorce but Caroline would not get her crown. She continued to petition for the right to take part in the coronation, but to no avail. On the day of the ceremony, in a scene right out of a movie, she turned up at the Westminster Abbey and went from door to door, demanding entrance, but was refused. One door was literally slammed in her face.

A few weeks later Caroline fell ill with what was probably intestinal obstruction. "I know I am dying they have killed me at last!" she said. She died on 7 August 1821 at the age of 53. George IV lived another nine years, but never remarried.

King George III 1738–1820

In 1765 King George III had suffered a breakdown. He was depressed, then cheerful, then depressed again. At first his doctors attributed his distress to a violent cold, which they treated by bleeding him. Weeks passed, and the king remained "sulky" and "agitated" and eventually seemed to recover.

There is dispute today about the cause of this illness and whether it was related to King George's later madness. However, in 1788 King George had another breakdown. He suffered fits of gloom alternating with excited spells during which he talked incessantly and behaved oddly at one point allegedly handing a visitor to the palace with a blank sheet of paper for no apparent reason. Again his physician, Sir George Baker, tried to cure him by bleeding him. When this failed, Baker concluded that the king's problem was more than physical. According to history, George was by turns depressed and agitated, and did and said things people found strange, but he had not taken leave of his senses. Indeed, some observers thought he was thinking more clearly than ever before. But he was not fit to rule, and no one understood what was wrong or how to help him.

A new set of physicians, Dr Francis Willis and his son John, arrived on the scene. The Willises confined the king to a straitjacket when they deemed it necessary, and gave him medicine to make him vomit when they felt his behaviour was getting out of hand, but on the whole they treated George more gently than other doctors had. The king began to get better, and within a few months he was able to resume his royal duties.Over the next twenty years King George suffered occasional brief relapses, but it wasn't until 1810 that he truly became the mad King George depicted in legend. The Prince of Wales was named Prince Regent and assumed the king's powers, and

George was relegated to the role of laughable lunatic. Wild stories were told about him, that he had addressed a tree as the King of Prussia, insisted on ending every sentence with the word "peacock", etc. etc. – and many of these stories were completely untrue. What is true is that he spent his last years deaf, blind, lonely and confused, talking to the ghosts of his dead children. He died in 1820 and the Prince Regent became King George IV.

Today it is widely believed that the king suffered from porphyria, a rare genetic disorder which interferes with the body's chemical balance. The symptoms include rashes, abdominal pain, and reddish blue urine, all of which George suffered. Untreated, it can affect the nervous system and lead to insanity. If King George were alive today, he would be treated with drugs and advised to avoid too much sunlight.

Grisly Tales from History
Purple Patch
Roman Empire

Only the Roman Emperor was allowed to wear the colour purple. If any ordinary person was seen wearing purple they were executed as a traitor.

Alfred the Great circa AD 849–AD 899

Alfred was born around AD 849, the youngest son of King
Athelwolf of Wessex. Little is known of Alfred's early life, and
much of what is believed about him comes from the writing of a
bishop named Asser, although some modern historians often
cast doubt on Asser's accuracy.

According to tradition, Alfred was sent as a child to Rome,
where the pope anointed him king, but in recent times this
version of the story is generally regarded as false. It is possible
however, that Alfred might have accompanied his father on a
pilgrimage to Rome. Alfred's mother died when Alfred was
young and his father remarried for political reasons. He angered
his subjects by making his new wife, Judith, queen at a time
when queens had been outlawed because of the actions of a
previous queen. Alfred's father seems to have lost his throne due
to this unpopular move. He abdicated in 855 and his eldest son,
Athelbald, became king.

In time, Alfred's other two brothers also inherited the throne.
After the death of the last surviving brother, Athelred, in 871,
the Witan chose Alfred to be king (skipping over Athelred's
sons, who were too young to rule). Despite a supposedly poor
early education and health problems that persisted throughout
his life, Alfred had become a great scholar and warrior. As
king he repeatedly defeated invading Vikings, promoted
religion and education, reformed the law, and paved the
way for his descendants to become the first kings of a united
England.

He is perhaps best remembered today for his legendary
encounter with a peasant woman who, not recognizing the king,
asked him to keep an eye on some cakes she was cooking and
then scolded him for absent-mindedly letting them burn.

Although it has to be noted, that like many of the stories

about Alfred, this may be the invention of later writers. Alfred
died on 26 October 899 and was succeeded by his son Edward
the Elder.

King found guilty – 3,000 years after the fact!
On 17 December 2006, a mock trial was held of King David, the
second monarch of the Israelites and a biblical hero, 3,000 years
after the event. The proceedings took place in an auditorium at
Baltimore Hebrew University. Facing charges of adultery,
murder, and coveting another man's wife, he maintained his
innocence on all counts.

Organizers said the event, which was part of the university's
Lifelong Learning programme, was intended to explore the
biblical account of the relationship between King David and
Bathsheba, a tawdry tale of an ancient love triangle that ends
badly for Bathsheba's husband, Uriah. In summary, the biblical
account of the story portrayed to the audience was that David,
attracted to a woman, found out the woman was named
Bathsheba and was married to one of his soldiers, Uriah. David
ignored that inconvenient fact and sent for her. She became
pregnant at a time when her husband was off laying siege to a
foreign city.

David later sent a message to his general, Joab: "Place Uriah
in the front line where the fighting is fiercest; then fall back so
he might be killed." Sure enough, Uriah was killed while
attacking the city of Rabbath. King David's defence was that he
was at his palace when Uriah was killed. In the end, the
audience voted and found David guilty on all three counts. The
Judge deferred handing down a sentence, as she thought God
had already taken care of that.

Biblical scholars believe David lived about 3,000 years ago.
He said the Bible portrays David as a heroic figure and beyond

reproach until the Second Book of Samuel, when from the roof of his palace in Jerusalem, the king spies a bathing beauty.

Humour was injected into the piece when Bathsheba took to the witness stand, David's lawyer called into question her motives for bathing where the king could see her. "You wanted to be queen, didn't you?" he charged.

"No."

"You wanted your son to be king, didn't you?"

"He was a good boy," Bathsheba is reported to have said with a shrug. "I wanted the best for him, as any good Jewish mother would." This apparently drew laughter from the audience.

Elizabeth I 1533–1603

Elizabeth I was glorified by poets and artists as Gloriana, the Virgin Queen. With the help of fine clothes, jewels, and cosmetics, the vain queen maintained a glamorous image despite her advancing age. In her mid-fifties she fell in love with Robert Devereux, Earl of Essex, son of Lettice Knollys. Essex was in his early twenties, good-looking, and extremely arrogant. Although he reigned as the queen's favourite for many years, he did not always show Elizabeth the deference she demanded. Once, when Elizabeth slapped him during an argument, Essex threatened to draw his sword on her. Elizabeth sent him to Ireland to quell a rebellion and while there, Essex ignored the queen's orders and pursued his own agenda. When he defied her by returning to England without permission, Elizabeth placed him under house arrest. After his release Essex attempted to lead an uprising against the queen, and the heartbroken Elizabeth had no choice but to sentence him to death. Essex was executed in 1601.

Two years later Elizabeth became very ill. Perhaps she did not want to live without Essex; when her doctors offered her medicine, she refused to take it. She died on 24 March 1603 at the age of 69. She was the last of the Tudor monarchs; her successor was Mary Queen of Scots' son, James.

Grisly Tales from History

Up Pompeii
Roman Empire

In AD 79, Mount Vesuvius erupted burying the citizens of Pompei. The hot dust and lava buried everything several metres deep and "froze" the bodies in the position of whatever they were doing at the time.

The Tarquin Dynasty, Rome circa 600 BC

At one time historians believed the Tarquins were purely mythological, but their existence is fairly widely accepted today. The first Tarquin king was a Greek noble who emigrated to Rome with his Etruscan wife and rose high in Roman society. He was called Lucius Tarquinius Priscus, or Tarquin the Elder. He became guardian of Ancus Marcius's sons and somehow seized the throne after the king's death in 616 BC. He reigned until 578 BC, when he was murdered by Ancus Marcius's sons and was succeeded by his son-in-law, Servius Tullius.

Servius may have been an Etruscan, or a Latin slave who was born into Priscus's household and later adopted by the king. He arranged for his daughters, both called Tullia, to marry two brothers who were Priscus's sons or grandsons. It was to prove to be a disaster and the undoing of King Servius. The couples were mismatched and one of the Tullias fell in love with her sister's husband, Lucius Tarquinius Superbus (Tarquin the Proud). Tullia and Tarquin both killed their spouses, married each other, and then, to top it all off, Tarquin killed old King Servius and Tullia deliberately drove over her father's corpse.

This diabolical couple had an equally despicable son name Sextus who brought about the downfall of the Tarquin dynasty when he raped a virtuous noblewoman named Lucretia. After making her father and husband and their friends promise to punish her attacker, she stabbed herself to death in front of them. True to their word, the men avenged her, overthrowing Tarquin, who went into exile. Sextus also fled the city, but was assassinated by old enemies. The monarchy was ended, and Rome became a republic in 509 BC.

Spanish Royalty
Spain's first twentieth century monarch was King Alfonso XIII (born 1886), whose attempts to dominate the government made him very unpopular with politicians and public alike. He survived several assassination attempts then went into exile in 1931 after the Republicans came to power. Although he did not abdicate, he never returned to Spain. He died in 1941.

Spain did not become a monarchy again until 1947, but it was not until 1975 that a new monarch, Alfonso XIII's grandson King Juan Carlos, ascended the throne. He continues to reign today, playing a mostly ceremonial role similar to the British monarchy. His wife, Queen Sofia, was born a Greek princess. The king and queen of Spain have two daughters, Princess Elena and Princess Cristina, and a son, Crown Prince Felipe, who is the heir to the throne. The prince married former television journalist Letizia Ortiz in 2004. They have two daughters

346

King Edward VII 1841–1900

Edward VII was the eldest son of Queen Victoria and Prince Albert. Born in 1841, he did not inherit the throne until his mother's death in 1901, when he was fifty-nine years old. Given little responsibility during Victoria's lifetime, Bertie (as his family called him) devoted himself to a life of pleasure. Despite his 1863 marriage to Princess Alexandra of Denmark, with whom he had six children, he was infamous for his many mistresses and playboy lifestyle. As king, Edward VII was popular with his people and abroad, but he reigned for only nine years before dying in 1910. His oldest surviving son, King George V, succeeded him.

Grisly Tales from History

Life in Rome

Roman Empire

Life expectancy in ancient Rome was not much over fifty. Many died very young because of disease. The poor often left new-born babies outside to die if they couldn't afford to feed them. It was also not uncommon to sell children as slaves. Although the Romans had some knowledge about the workings of the human body they had no such things as painkillers or anaesthetics and operations were performed while the patient was still conscious. They did however, know the healing power of garlic and herbs and ate a lot of them along with large quantities of olive oil.

The Madness of King Charles II 1630–1685

As a reward for his assistance to Cromwell in the English Civil War, Thomas Blood was awarded a small English estate. However, five years later, when the monarchy was reinstated and King Charles II held the throne, the Duke of Ormand usurped Blood's land. Furious, Blood plotted to murder him. The plot failed and Blood subsequently had a £1,000 bounty on his head. Afraid for his life, he fled to London. There he befriended the deputy keeper of the crown jewels (Talbot Edwards), seduced his daughter and convinced her to help him steal the crown jewels.

In 1671 Blood stabbed Talbot Edwards and stole a large collection of state jewels that included the king's crown. Edwards, though wounded did not die and sounded the alarm. Blood, was arrested on a nearby wharf by the River Thames. Incredibly, Charles II, the new monarch, not only returned Blood's land to him, but also threw a royal pardon and a £500 pension into the bargain!

King Henry VIII 1491–1547

According to historical anecdote, Henry VIII enlisted a nobleman to serve as his ambassador to King Francis I of France. His appointee was not happy with his new job because relations between the two countries were not good at the time. One day, as the nobleman recorded an aggressive message to be relayed to the French king from Henry VIII he begged to be excused. He feared that the infamously hot-tempered king might have him executed if he deigned to deliver it.

Henry is said to have reassured him, pointing out that if Francis killed him, there were dozens of Frenchmen in England whose heads Henry could lop off. Legend has it that the ambassador replied, "But of all these heads, there may not be one to fit my shoulders."

Queen Elizabeth I 1533–1603

Elizabeth I was rumoured to have had a court jester named
Master Pace. Apparently, unlike the rest of the court, he was
permitted to say outrageous things as long as they made the
queen laugh. Apparently, Pace once over-stepped the bounds of
propriety and was subsequently banished from the court for
insulting the queen before an important group of foreign
dignitaries.

However, fortunately, some time later, the Elizabeth
welcomed him back into the royal court, "Come now, Pace," she
is alleged to have said, "let us hear no more of our faults."

"No indeed, Madam," he agreed, "For I myself never talk of
what is discussed by all the world."

Nell Eleanor Gwyn, English actress, mistress of Charles II
1650–1687

Nell Gwyn, is famously known as the favourite mistress of King
Charles II. Apparently she made many enemies who are said to
have envied her in being the King's Concubine. It is said that
this never bothered Nell and that she always stood her ground
and came off well. She is alleged to have once had a falling out
with the Duchess of Portsmouth. They are said to have had a
catfight in which both ended up scrapping on the floor. During
the fight Nell apparently took a candle to the Duchess's hair and
set fire to it!

Grisly Tales from History

The Ratcliffe Highway Murders

19th Century

In 1811, on the Ratcliffe Highway in the East End of London, a Mr Marr, the owner of a lace warehouse, was murdered in his home along with his wife and baby and a shop boy. Twelve days later, along the same stretch of road, a Mr Williamson, the landlord of the King's Arms public house was murdered along with his wife and a female servant. These murders sparked panic and a demand for vengeance. To assuage this, the Home Secretary allowed the body of the suspected killer John Williams, who had hanged himself the night before his arrest, to be paraded through the East End. His body was then buried with a stake through his heart at the intersection of Commercial Road and Cannon Street.

Prince Charles 1948–

A famous rumour has it that during a hospital visit one day, Prince Charles was asked for a urine sample. It is said that Charles dutifully complied but had his valet hold the specimen bottle while he did his business!

Queen Mary, British Queen and wife of King George V
1867–1953

Queen Mary was once given a Russian icon which was of unknown origin but very beautiful. She requested that someone attempt to discover its origin and someone in her household remembered a Russian princess, cousin of the British Royal family who had escaped to London from the Bolshevik revolution in 1917. The said princess was duly invited to the palace for tea. Since living in exile the Russian princess had lived a life of relative poverty and obscurity but she recognized the icon as belonging to herself.

She recalled that it had been given to her at her baptism, had said her prayers to it every night and had saved it as she fled from her burning house in which her parents, brothers and sisters had been killed. She apparently told Queen Mary that she had been forced to sell it because she had become so poor. The queen is rumoured to have replied "I see, thank you so much for identifying it."

William the Conqueror circa 1028–1087

According to legend, as he led his men ashore at Pevensey during the conquest of England, William stumbled and fell. As his horrified men cursed the bad omen, the quick-witted William rose with a handful of soil to return the men's thoughts in a more positive direction.

He is said to have stood up clutching two handfuls of the soil beneath him and declared, "By the splendour of God, I have taken possession of my realm. The earth of England is in my two hands."

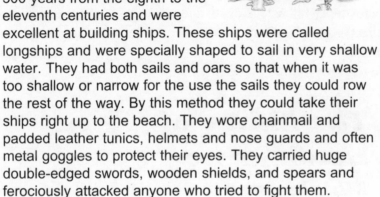

At Sea with the Vikings

Middle Ages

The Vikings were around for about 300 years from the eighth to the eleventh centuries and were excellent at building ships. These ships were called longships and were specially shaped to sail in very shallow water. They had both sails and oars so that when it was too shallow or narrow for the use the sails they could row the rest of the way. By this method they could take their ships right up to the beach. They wore chainmail and padded leather tunics, helmets and nose guards and often metal goggles to protect their eyes. They carried huge double-edged swords, wooden shields, and spears and ferociously attacked anyone who tried to fight them.

Augustus Gaius Julius Caesar Octavianus, Roman Emperor

63 BC–AD 14

Have you ever wondered why February has only twenty-eight days? Well, it is said that in 8 BC, the Roman Emperor Augustus renamed the thirty-day month of Sextilis (August) in his honor. Apparently still unsatisfied, he removed a day from February and added it to August, so that his own month would have as many days as Julius Caesar's (July).

Prince Albert, Prince Consort of Great Britain, husband of Queen Victoria 1819–1961

It is said that Prince Albert, husband of Queen Victoria, had much difficulty staying up beyond his usual bedtime. Apparently, during a Buckingham Palace concert attended by a large collection of very distinguished guests, Queen Victoria, realizing that her husband had fallen asleep, gently nudged him with her elbow.

The prince awoke, smiled at the ongoing performance, and then simply fell asleep again. Queen Victoria did the same thing with the same result over and over again for the rest of the evening!

Grisly Tales from History
The Abbey of Lindisfarne
Middle Ages

One of the Vikings earliest attacks on Britain was in AD 793. They arrived at the island of Lindisfarne in Scotland. The island had a castle and an abbey but the only inhabitants were monks. The Vikings killed most of the monks. The rest they beat and captured to be sold as slaves. After that they kicked the buildings to bits and stole all the treasure from the abbey at a time when religious places were seen as sacred.

Future Bingo

The future history of the world is hard to predict. But as we look forward in fear and hope, why not have some fun while we're waiting?

Keep this **Future Bingo** sheet to hand, and cross off any events that actually happen in the future. If you get a full page of amazing future events, then shout out "House".

If you send the finished page to the **Future Bingo** corporation (at an address yet to be determined), you may even receive a mystery prize . . .

New US capital city, Albuquerque.	Middle East peace process succeeds.
Randy Newman composes new national anthem.	"I was just talking gibberish," admits French philosopher.
King of Africa knights his favourite horse.	California declared illegal substance.

Chapter Twenty-three

Weird News: Death in Hammersmith

It was 1803 and the citizens of Hammersmith were all very worried. One of the local residents had recently been brutally murdered and the body had been recovered with the throat violently slit. They were convinced that the spirit of the murdered man was roaming along the banks of the River Thames, a ghost of his former self. Tales abounded of sightings of the terrifying, white monster with its horns and its howling shrieks. One woman went out for a walk, caught sight of the dreaded creature and instantaneously died of fright.

Two locals, Mr Smith, a highly respected customs officer, and his friend Mr Girdler, the neighbourhood watchman, were determined to form a vigilante group and rid their streets of this terrible threat. Mr Thomas Millwood was a bricklayer. On the evening of 3 January 1804 he went to visit his parents, who happened to live in Hammersmith, on his way home from work. By the time he left it was quite late and he was still wearing his normal work uniform which consisted of long white trousers and a white shirt. Mr Smith and Mr Girdler were on their night-watch when they caught sight of a ghostly white spectre ambling slowly along the banks of the Thames. They immediately concluded that this must be their prey and challenged the ghost to fight them. Being a peaceable soul, mistakenly assuming that he had just encountered two drunken men also on their way home, Mr Millwood decided to turn the other cheek and, ignoring their shouts, he walked on. Mr Smith panicked and shot Mr Millwood who collapsed dead in front of him. Seeing the blood, Mr Smith immediately realized his terrible mistake and surrendered himself to a passing wine merchant.

A mere ten days later he was up in the dock at the Old Bailey accused of murder. Many of the good citizens of Hammersmith came to give evidence about the terrifying reputation of the ghost. Mr Girdler told the jury at great length that Mr Smith was a generous and kind man and one of the best friends he had ever had. Mr Smith himself made a short but moving speech explaining that, whatever he had done, he had done it with the interests of his beloved Hammersmith at heart. The judge, in his summing up, explained to the jury that if they were satisfied that Mr Smith had shot the victim intentionally then he was guilty and there was no defence which could save him. He mistakenly ignored the possibility that Mr Smith might have had the intention to shoot a ghost but certainly not a man. The jury had no choice but to convict. The accused was sentenced immediately to death on the following Monday with his body to be given to surgeons for medical experiments.

Fortunately for Mr Smith a pardon arrived in the nick of time. But the bricklayers of Hammersmith were thereafter very careful always to change into their own clothes before they went home from work.

The Viking Thing

Middle Ages

The Vikings socialized at a gathering called the Thing. Here they could all have the chance to get off their chest anything that was bothering them. They also sorted out their arguments there as well. If a disagreement couldn't be sorted out at the Thing they had something else they called Ordeals. At Ordeals both parties of the argument would try to prove they were right. They proved their righteousness by walking over hot coals or boiling themselves alive because they believed that the gods would look after them if they were innocent.

Future Bingo

The future history of the world is hard to predict. But as we look forward in fear and hope, why not have some fun while we're waiting?

Keep this **Future Bingo** sheet to hand, and cross off any events that actually happen in the future. If you get a full page of amazing future events, then shout out "House".

If you send the finished page to the **Future Bingo** corporation (at an address yet to be determined), you may even receive a mystery prize . . .

Ghosts and zombies sign peace accord.	Loaf of bread price passes the million pound mark.
Banks say, "Don't worry about paying back mortgages, we don't really need the money."	Genetically modified asparagus annex Belgium, declare vegetable law.
National Association of Pet Cats decide it's time they did a bit more work about the house.	America adopts new emblem, The Foxtrotting Raccoon.

Chapter Twenty-four

Yet More Religious Mania

Mark Twain 1835–1910

Born Samuel Langhorne Clemens, Mark Twain was an American humourist, writer, and lecturer. A businessman, renowned for his ruthlessness, is said to have made a vow in the presence of Mark Twain. He apparently declared that before he died he intended to make a pilgrimage to the Holy Land and climb Mount Sinai to read the Ten Commandments aloud at the top. Twain is said to have replied. "It would be better if you could stay home in Boston and keep them."

Andrew Carnegie 1835–1919

During his lifetime, Andrew Carnegie, the Scottish-born American steel magnate and philanthropist endowed 2,811 libraries and many charitable foundations as well as the internationally famous Carnegie Endowment for International Peace. He also bought 7,689 organs for churches. He is supposed to have said that they were, "To lessen the pain of the sermons."

Phillips Brooks 1835–1893

As he recovered from a serious illness, American Episcopal bishop Phillips Brooks ordered that no visitors be allowed to see him – not even his closest friends. However, when the agnostic Robert Ingersoll called, the bishop welcomed him with divine grace. When Ingersoll was informed of the privilege, he supposedly asked Brooks why he had made an exception in his case. Brooks is reported to have replied "I feel confident of seeing my friends in the next world but this may be my last chance of seeing you."

Grisly Tales from History
The Ice Pick Method
Middle Ages

In the thirteenth century, priests in Europe treated loonies with beatings and force-feedings of blood and sheep dung to exorcise evil spirits. Between 1790 and 1813, American physician Benjamin Rush whirled clinically depressed patients around at high speeds before submerging them in water. In the late 1940s, Walter Freeman developed a ten-minute procedure to scramble the frontal lobes of the insane – by jamming an ice pick through their eye sockets.

Dwight Lyman Moody 1837–1899

While British evangelist Dwight Lyman Moody was attending a convention in Indianapolis, he reportedly asked his song leader Ira Sankey to meet him at six o'clock one evening by a certain street corner. When Sankey arrived, Mr Moody requested that he stand on a box and sing. A crowd gathered and Moody spoke briefly to them then invited the people to follow him to the nearby convention hall. Soon the auditorium was filled with people, and Moody began to preach the gospel to them.

When the convention delegates began to arrive, Moody stopped preaching and is rumoured to have said, "Now we must close, as the brethren of the convention wish to come and discuss the topic: How to reach the masses."

Edward VII 1841–1910
Edward VII, the eldest son of Queen Victoria and Albert, was
King of Great Britain and Ireland from 1901 to 1910. During
Queen Victoria's Diamond Jubilee in 1897, her son Edward was
often called upon to represent her at public events. Apparently,
on one such occasion, hearing mention of the popular hymn
"Eternal Father, Strong to Save," Edward is said to have
complained, "It's all very well about the Eternal Father, but
what about my eternal mother?"

William Archibald Spooner 1844–1930
During his tenure as Warden of New College, Oxford, between
1903 and 1924, William Spooner was asked whether there were
many Christian Socialists at the college. He is said to have
replied that in his estimation, there were only two: Dr Rashdall
(a clerical Fellow) and himself. However, he continued to
explain that he wasn't much of a socialist and Dr Rashdall
wasn't much of a Christian.

Abbe Arthur Mugnier 1853–1944
Someone once asked the Abbe Mugnier whether or not he
believed in hell. He is said to have replied, "Yes, because it is a
dogma of the church, but I don't believe there is anyone in it."

Grisly Tales from History

Shopping for Teeth

Middle Ages

In the thirteenth century, if you had toothache you were taken to the market place where the offending tooth was pulled out with a pair of pliers, without anaesthetic or painkillers.

Oscar Wilde 1854–1900

Oscar Wilde was an Irish aesthete, wit, and writer, noted for his scandalous affair with Lord Douglas of Queensbury and his subsequent trial and imprisonment, for sodomy.

While still a young student at Oxford, Oscar Wilde arrived late for an examination in "Rudiments of Faith and Religion." He then made things worse by failing to show the contrition expected by his examiners who were all learned men of the cloth, chief among them a nephew of the Archbishop of Canterbury, Dr William Spooner. A contemporary of Wilde, Douglas Sladen, later recalled that the examiners were so appalled that they gave him a Bible and told him to copy out the long twenty-seventh chapter of the Acts. Apparently, Wilde copied it out in such beautiful handwriting that their hearts relented, and they told him that he need not write out any more. Half an hour later they noticed that he was still copying it out. They pointed out that he could now stop writing. He is said to have replied that he was so interested in the subject matter that he could not leave off. It was about a man named Paul, who went on a voyage, and was caught in a terrible storm. "I was afraid that he would be drowned, but, do you know, Mr Spooner, he was saved, and when I found he was saved, I thought of coming to tell you!"

George Bernard Shaw 1856–1950
George Bernard Shaw was an Anglo–Irish socialist, playwright, critic, wit, and man of letters, who won the Nobel Prize for Literature in 1925. He and Annie Besant disagreed about things religious. "I delivered myself of an unbounded denunciation of Theosophy," Shaw recalled of one disagreement. "Mrs Annie Besant listened to me with complete and genuine amusement and then said she had become a vegetarian (as I was) and that perhaps it had enfeebled her mind."

André Gide 1869–1951
André Gide was a French novelist and a prominent liberal thinker, who was awarded the Nobel Prize for Literature in 1947. Several days after his death on 19 February 1951, a curious telegram, bearing Gide's signature, appeared on a bulletin board in the Sorbonne: "Hell doesn't exist," the notice read. "Better notify Claudel." The mystic poet Paul Claudel apparently once unsuccessfully attempted to convert the André Gide to his Catholic faith.

Grisly Tales from History
What's Your Poison?
Middle Ages

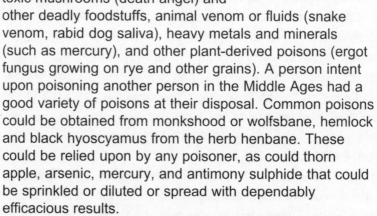

A medieval poisoner had a variety
of options: deadly herbs (henbane),
toxic mushrooms (death angel) and
other deadly foodstuffs, animal venom or fluids (snake
venom, rabid dog saliva), heavy metals and minerals
(such as mercury), and other plant-derived poisons (ergot
fungus growing on rye and other grains). A person intent
upon poisoning another person in the Middle Ages had a
good variety of poisons at their disposal. Common poisons
could be obtained from monkshood or wolfsbane, hemlock
and black hyoscyamus from the herb henbane. These
could be relied upon by any poisoner, as could thorn
apple, arsenic, mercury, and antimony sulphide that could
be sprinkled or diluted or spread with dependably
efficacious results.

The simplest method of poisoning someone, was to add
a single or compound poison to a highly spiced and/or
chopped dish or in a victim's glass of wine. The strong
flavours and uneven texture would mask the bitter taste
and consistency of the poison.

Joseph Hilaire Pierre Belloc 1870–1953

Hilaire Belloc was a French-born English writer, poet, satirist, historian, and politician. Bertrand Russell, at dinner at Trinity College, Cambridge, reportedly told him the story of a chapel he had been in where the Ten Commandments were scrawled on two boards and placed where the congregation could read them. Belloc, who vehemently disagreed with Russell's liberal views on marriage, is said to have remarked, "I always think, when I see boards like that, that there should be a third board over them." And what would this third board say, Russell wanted to know? "Candidates," Belloc explained, "should not attempt more than six of these."

Warren Austin 1877–1962

One day in 1948, Warren Austin, America's Ambassador to the United Nations, urged the warring Muslim Arabs and Jewish Israelis to sit down and settle their differences . . . "like good Christians."

Joseph Hilaire Pierre Belloc 1870–1953

Hilaire Belloc knew that his Roman Catholicism could present political problems, however, he confronted religious prejudice and sought election as a British MP in 1906. On the occasion of his first speech, at Salford, Belloc appeared on the rostrum – rosary in hand – and is alleged to have made the following declaration: "I am a Catholic. As far as possible I go to Mass every day. As far as possible I kneel down and tell these beads every day . . . If you reject me on account of my religion, I shall thank God that he has spared me the indignity of being your representative." Belloc was elected.

John Calvin Coolidge 1872–1933

Calvin Coolidge, known as "Silent Cal", was a Republican, the thirtieth president of the USA between 1923 and 1929. As he returned from church one day, Calvin Coolidge's father supposedly asked him on what topic the minister had preached. "Sin," Coolidge replied. His father wanted to know what the minister had said about sin. Coolidge is said to have responded: "He was against it." It has to be noted that Coolidge himself denied this story.

Grisly Tales from History

Burying the Bones

Middle Ages

In medieval China, at appointed times of the year, officials buried abandoned corpses, and in order to banish agents of death and disease, communities held rites for "hungry ghosts." For the medieval Chinese, death turned the living into bones, ghosts, and memories. It was important to reconcile and attempt to harness the volatile schism between these states and even more so when the corpses were unaccounted for or abandoned. Strategies often involved exorcism.

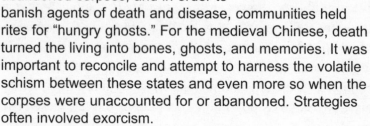

Pope John XXIII 1881–1963
Angelo Roncalli, the papal nuncio to France, and later to be
Pope John XXII, was once invited to a formal banquet. It is
reported that his dinner companion wore an extremely low-cut
dress, which the prelate pretended not to notice. However, when
dessert was served he allegedly selected a plump apple and
offered it to the woman, who politely declined. "Please take it,
madam," he supposedly pleaded. "It was only after Eve ate the
apple that she became aware of how little she had on."

Ronald Knox 1888–1957
Ronald Knox was a Roman Catholic priest and author, who was
appointed Chaplain of Oxford University in 1926. He apparently
once found himself embroiled in a theological argument with the
scientist John Scott Haldane. Haldane is said to have asked
Knox "In a universe containing millions of planets, is it not
inevitable that life should appear on at least one of them?"
   Knox replied, "Sir, if Scotland Yard found a body in your
cabin trunk, would you say to them: "There are millions of
trunks in the world – surely one of them must contain a body?" I
think they would still want to know who put it there!"

Sir Alfred Joseph Hitchcock 1889–1980
According to rumour, the famous British film director, Alfred
Hitchcock suddenly pointed through the window while driving
through a Swiss village one day. "That," he is said to have
declared, "is the most frightening sight I have ever seen."
Hitchcock's fellow-traveler could see nothing more alarming
than a priest talking to a small boy, his hand resting on the
young boy's shoulder. "Run, little boy, run!" Hitchcock
apparently cried, poking his head through the window. "Run for
your life!" (Hitchcock, at the time, was a practising Catholic.)

Grisly Tales from History
To Hell and Back
Middle Ages

It seems that people had near-death experiences during the middle ages too. In one story a hermit was revived from death and testified that he had been to hell. Apparently he saw several powerful men dangling in fire. He says that just as he too was being dragged into the flames, an angel in a shining garment came to his rescue and sent him back to life with the words "Leave, and consider carefully how you will live from now on." According to folklore, after his return to life, the hermit took to fasting and praying, He was convinced that he had indeed seen the terrors of hell.

George Simon Kaufman 1889–1961

George S. Kaufman, the American playwright, director, journalist, and wit, while lunching at the Algonquin Hotel one afternoon, was subjected by a notorious bore to a lengthy monologue on the great antiquity and eminence of his family – which, the man claimed, could trace its origins back to the Crusades. "I had a famous ancestor, too," Kaufman is said to have deadpanned, "Sir Roderick Kaufman. He also went off to the Crusades." Here Kaufman paused for a moment, before adding: "As a spy, of course."

Francis Joseph Spellman 1889–1967
Francis Spellman was an American Roman Catholic cardinal
from 1946, popularly known as "The American Pope". He
once presented a recently appointed Grand Knight of the
Knights of Columbus with a medallion of Pope John XXIII as a
token of appreciation for his generous donation to the Roman
Catholic Church. Apparently, during the ceremony, the nervous
Knight dropped the medallion and, bending down to retrieve it,
was amused to hear the cardinal's whispered commentary:
"Heads!"

Julius Henry "Groucho" Marx 1895–1977
One day, Groucho Marx was descending in the elevator at the
Hotel Danieli in Venice when it stopped on another floor to
admit a group of priests. One of these, recognizing Groucho,
told him that his mother was a great fan. Groucho is said to have
replied, "I didn't know you guys were allowed to have
mothers."

On another occasion, Groucho met another priest while
visiting Montreal. "Groucho," the priest apparently declared,
trying to shake his hand, "I want to thank you for all the joy
you've put in the world." "Thank you, Father," Groucho
replied. "And I want to thank you for all the joy you've taken
out of it!"

Grisly Tales from History
Burn
Middle Ages

In medieval warfare, the siege
predominated: for every battle,
there were hundreds of sieges.
This is one of the reasons that
there is so little documentation of
the period. Sieges often involved burning everything to the
ground.

Joseph Randolph Ackerley 1896–1967

Joseph Ackerley was a British poet and writer, the literary editor
of the *BBC Magazine*. On a sandwich board being carried in
Regent Street by a young man were the words, "Are you lost, or
eternally saved?" Ackerley frowned at it because he felt it
wasn't really right to ask such intimate questions in public.
However, apparently the young man smiled at the poet and said.
"It's all right, it ain't meant for you."

Frederick William Densham

While the Rev. Frederick William Densham was the incumbent
at Warleggan, Cornwall, from 1931 to 1953, few people
attended his church; often no one at all came. When no one

came to church he would lock it up and go to the Methodist Chapel. After years of non-attendance at church by his parishioners his entries in the Service Book would apparently often read, "No fog, no wind, no rain, no congregation." In desperation, he cut out figures in wood and cardboard and fixed them to the pews. Apparently, these figures, which he named after all the rectors at Warleggen, were preached to, offered the sacraments, and given absolution.

Andrew Agnellus 1908–1987
The English Franciscan Father Andrew Agnellus, at the time the UK BBC TV channel's adviser on Roman Catholic affairs, received a letter from a producer asking how he might ascertain the official Roman Catholic view of heaven and hell. Andrew answered him in a memorandum comprising a single word: "Die."

Francis Henry Compton Crick 1916–2004
 Francis Crick was a British biologist, a Nobel Prize recipient for Medicine, in 1962, noted for his discovery, with James D. Watson, of the molecular double helix spiral structure of DNA. When his Cambridge college began the construction of a chapel in 1961, he promptly resigned. Shortly afterwards, he received a conciliatory letter from Winston Churchill, who supposedly pointed out that the mere existence of a chapel should be of no consequence, as no one would be required to enter it against his will.

Crick's reply to Churchill, along with ten guineas, apparently proposed the construction of a brothel, and hastened to point out that its mere existence should be of no consequence, as no one would be required to enter it against his will.

Grisly Tales from History
Baptism
Before Birth
Middle Ages

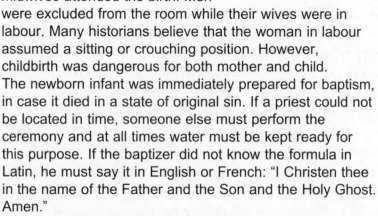

In cities, villages and noble houses,
babies were born at home and
midwives attended the birth. Men
were excluded from the room while their wives were in
labour. Many historians believe that the woman in labour
assumed a sitting or crouching position. However,
childbirth was dangerous for both mother and child.

The newborn infant was immediately prepared for baptism,
in case it died in a state of original sin. If a priest could not
be located in time, someone else must perform the
ceremony and at all times water must be kept ready for
this purpose. If the baptizer did not know the formula in
Latin, he must say it in English or French: "I Christen thee
in the name of the Father and the Son and the Holy Ghost.
Amen."

The words must be said in the right order. For example,
if the baptizer said, "In the name of the Son and the Father
and the Holy Ghost," the sacrament was invalid. Many
babies were baptized as soon as their head and shoulders
appeared during the birth process with the rest of their
bodies still inside the mother.

Pope John Paul II 1920–2005
The Pole Karol Wojtyla, became Pope John Paul II in 1978. His
new car was reported on by Craig Kilborn in December 1999 in
the following way: "The Pope's new Fiat, which can withstand
direct machine gun fire, was designed for John Tesh [the
American pianist, composer of New Age and contemporary
Christian music, and nationally syndicated radio host]. The Pope
will use the $1.3 million car to fulfill one of his duties, waving
at the poor."

Brendan Behan 1923–1964
Brendan Behan was an Irish playwright, noted for his affiliation
with the Irish Republican Army from 1937. There is a rumour
that just before he died, Behan looked up at the nun who was
taking his pulse and said, with a smile, "Bless you, Sister! May
all your sons be bishops!"

Charlton Heston 1924–
When, in 1965, Charlton Heston appeared as John the Baptist in
George Stevens' biblical epic *The Greatest Story Ever Told*, the
film's baptism scene was shot on the Colorado River – in
November. In the film Heston duly stood in the river and
baptized dozens of locals who had been invited to play Christian
converts in the film. "It was lovely to see when it finally came
to their turn," he is said to have recalled. "They'd step into the
water and you'd see this expression of what I trust came across
as ecstasy on their faces." In fact, the water was so cold that
some of the extras nearly lost consciousness.

Marion G. "Pat" Robertson 1930–

In 1985, as Hurricane Gloria was on its way towards the United States eastern coast, televangelist Pat Robertson went on air to pray. "In the name of Jesus," he apparently declared, "we command you to stop where you are and move northeast, away from land, and away from harm."

Incredible as it seems, the hurricane did, in fact, seem to begin to head north-eastwards. Publicly, Robertson's claims to have changed the direction of the hurricane were met with considerable scorn. Particularly in Long Island – which lies to the north-east of Robertson's native Virginia and which was devastated by Gloria after the hurricane changed course.

Grisly Tales from History

Spanish Soap
Middle Ages

Soap was most likely invented in the Orient and brought to the Western world early in the Middle Ages. It was made in workshops, of accumulated mutton fat, wood ash, or potash, and natural soda and had a soft texture like grease. Hard soaps appeared in the twelfth century. They were luxury articles, made of olive oil, soda, and a little lime, often with aromatic herbs. They were manufactured in the olive-growing south, especially Spain; hence the modern Castile soap. Only the very wealthy could afford such soap.

Sandy Koufax 1935–
Shortly after joining the Los Angeles Dodgers, Sandy Koufax
(born Sanford) attended a pig roast party at the home of fellow
Dodger team mate Duke Snider. Snider's wife, felt that Koufax
(being Jewish) might feel out of place at a pig roast, and did her
best to put him at ease. She asked him "What would you like to
eat?" Apparently, Koufax, simply pointed at the roasting pig and
replied, "I'll have some of that turkey!"

Fred Silverman 1937–
A friend of CBS president Fred Silverman once asked whether
he planned to go home for the Yom Kippur holiday. Silverman
wanted to know on which day Yom Kippur would fall.
"Wednesday," said his friend. "Wednesday?" Silverman is
alleged to have said. "You mean they've scheduled Yom Kippur
opposite *Charlie's Angels*?"

Saddam Hussein 1937–2006
It is said that the late Iraqi President Saddam Hussein, who was
executed in 2006, once had a 600-page copy of the Koran
handwritten in his own blood. "For once," one commentator is
reported to have remarked, "I wish that the Koran were a little
longer." Until Saddam's demise, his Koran was housed in a
mosque in Western Baghdad built to celebrate his "victory" in
the First Gulf War. The mosque's name? "Mother of All Battles
Mosque."

Muhammad Ali 1942–
The American boxer Muhammad Ali (formerly Cassius Clay)
was World Heavyweight Boxing Champion from 1964 to 1971,
from 1974 to 1978, and from 1978 to 1980. When asked by
reporters about his conversion to Islam, he is said to have joked
that he was going to have four wives: one to shine his shoes, one
to feed him grapes, one to rub oil on his muscles – and one
named Peaches.

John Ashcroft 1942–
During a Justice Department meeting, Attorney-General John
Ashcroft apparently claimed that God was "working for" his
wife Janet. Apparently, she had recently been bumped off a
flight by an airline – and had been rewarded with extra frequent-
flier miles and a free ticket. Ashcroft is also rumoured to have
explained that Christianity had its limits. "The law is not about
forgiveness," he is supposed to have said. "It is oftentimes about
vengeance, oftentimes about revenge."

Ronald Thiemann 20th Century
Ronald Thiemann, the Dean of Harvard's Divinity School,
called the university's technical support department one day in
May 1999, to request more disk space on a computer in an
office at his Harvard-owned residence. Technicians reportedly
soon found the cause of the problem. Apparently, the dean had
been downloading and storing thousands of pornographic
images. Thiemann was asked to resign his post (for "conduct
unbecoming a dean"), but he remained a tenured faculty
member. One of his accomplishments after his resignation, was
the creation of the school's Center for the Study of Values in
Public Life.

Fighting Girls
Middle Ages

It is a little known fact that women fought in battles from the tenth to the seventeenth centuries. It has always been assumed that the women who did fight were only doing so in defence of homes during desperate circumstances or for religious reasons (like Joan of Arc). In the European middle ages, war was the main activity in which masculinity was demonstrated. However, by the end of the eleventh century, women fighters are mentioned in the chronicles. In the later Middle Ages women fighters were written about as wondrous oddities.

There is documented evidence that women fought in defence of homes, of aggressive women and women who made a lifestyle of warfare for personal or religious reasons, warrior queens or great women leaders. Usually peasant women or minor nobility, aggressive women were often frowned upon as they were seen to be out of place, and presumptuous.

In 1640, several young ladies in Provence and Paris fought duels out of spite and jealousy. They fought in the streets and aimed their blows at each other's faces and breasts!

Zarqa Nawaz 20th Century

Zarqa Nawaz is a Canadian film director, noted for such films as *Death Threat* (1998*)*and *BBQ Muslims* (1996). Irritated that Muslims seemed to be being blamed for the Oklahoma City bombing in 1995, she began to write and direct so-called "terrody" films (comedies about terrorism) with the aim of deflating Muslim stereotypes. She also set up a production company called *Fun*damentalist Films . It's motto was to "put the fun back into fundamentalism."

Deacon Evans 20th Century

A Welsh revivalist preacher once swept to his conclusion by asking everyone in the congregation who wished to go to heaven to raise their hands. Everyone did, with the exception of Deacon Evans, prominently seated in the very first row. Apparently the affronted preacher remarked to Mr Evans, "Surely you want to go to heaven?" Evans supposedly replied "Yes, but not by the excursion train."

Grisly Tales from History

Choose Your Parliament

Middle Ages

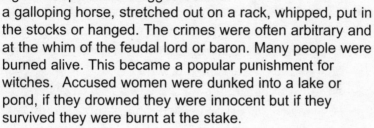

There were many kinds of inventive punishment during the Middle Ages. People were dragged behind a galloping horse, stretched out on a rack, whipped, put in the stocks or hanged. The crimes were often arbitrary and at the whim of the feudal lord or baron. Many people were burned alive. This became a popular punishment for witches. Accused women were dunked into a lake or pond, if they drowned they were innocent but if they survived they were burnt at the stake.

Chapter Twenty-five

Weird News: Living on a Tightrope

Henri Rochatain, who once walked 4,000 miles around France on a pair of stilts, subsequently pulled off an even more amazing feat: for six months he lived on a tightrope – literally. For half a year he ate, exercised and even slept on a stretch of rope suspended eighty-two feet above a supermarket car park in St Etienne, France, without once coming down. His only articles of furniture were a covered toilet and a board bed. These were not attached to anything; while in use they were simply balanced on the rope. He had no defence against the elements and lived on a diet of seaweed soup, biscuits, and tea.

Scientists were amazed by his endurance. "It is fantastic that he managed to sleep at all," said Dr Paul Monet, whose team monitored Rochatain's nervous system through electrodes attached to his skin. "He slept well even in thunderstorms and high winds. It is quite astonishing that he could rest, knowing that if he turned over in the night he would plunge off the rope."

M. Rochatain passed the time by walking up and down, doing stunts like standing on his head and occasionally pretending to fall off. He was not just in it for the thrills and the scientific discovery though. The owner of the supermarket over which he was perched paid him a large fee for attracting so many onlookers/customers.

Clean Shave
Middle Ages

Shaving in the Middle Ages was difficult, painful, and infrequent because the soap was inefficient and the razors, which looked like carving knives, were likely to be old and dull. Even haircutting was a disagreeable experience. Scissors were similar to grass trimming shears; they must have pulled mightily. By the thirteenth century some aristocrats had toothbrushes although cleaning the teeth was generally accomplished by rubbing with a green hazel twig and wiping with a woollen cloth.

Future Bingo

The future history of the world is hard to predict. But as we look forward in fear and hope, why not have some fun while we're waiting?

Keep this **Future Bingo** sheet to hand, and cross off any events that actually happen in the future. If you get a full page of amazing future events, then shout out "House".

If you send the finished page to the **Future Bingo** corporation (at an address yet to be determined), you may even receive a mystery prize . . .

"We're too darned rich," admit investment bankers.	First ex-wrestler to be elected President.
Lunatics take over the asylum.	Landlord fixes dripping tap.
Tapdancing movies come back into vogue.	Evil genius steals vowels from world's keyboards, demands $1 billion ransom.